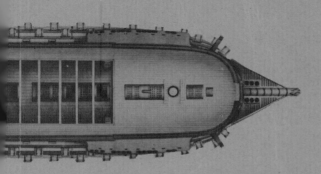

120 Guns
Keel laid down in
H.M. Dockyard Woolwich
14th November 1809
Launched 20th June 1814
Commissioner
C Cunningham Esq
Master Shipwright
E Sison Esq

Ship modelling hints & tips.

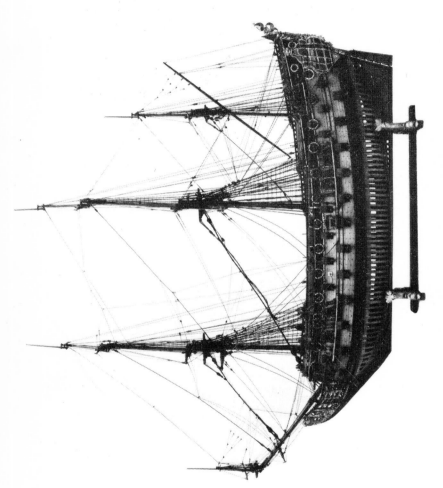

St. Michael 1669   *Picture by National Maritime Museum*

Ship modelling hints & tips.

by Lt. Cdr. J H Craine, R.N.R.
(retired) *Jason*
Edited by John L Bowen

ARCO PUBLISHING COMPANY, INC
New York

© Conway Maritime Press

First Published 1948
Second (revised) Edition 1973
Published by Arco Publishing Company, Inc.
219 Park Avenue South,
New York, N.Y. 10003
ISBN 0 668 03348 7
Library of Congress Catalog Card Number 73-81385

Cover Illustrations

Front Cover: Large, rigged model of *H.M. Bark Endeavour*
Courtesy of National Maritime Museum
Back Cover: Top. Yacht model of 1690. Sails and rigging are modern, but spars and hull are contemporary.
Courtesy of National Maritime Museum
Bottom. Model of Anson's *Centurion*, made in 1747
Courtesy of Arthur L Tucker.

Cover by Martin Treadway Design
Designed by Jon Blackmore
Illustrations by G Campbell
Printing Printed in Great Britain

Preface

THIS is not a book to guide you specially on one particular model, but rather to be of some help to you in making any model. It must, however, be *your* inspiration, it must be *your* choice of ship and above all, it must be *your* will—to complete the model. Given these, this book should be an encouragement over vexatious obstacles, a light to peer into dark places, an introduction to worthy friends, a counsellor in the search for truth, a shopper in the highways and byways for the best materials, and, at all times, a kindly critic.

It may be that in the years to come your knowledge and skill will go far beyond the limits of these pages. Nevertheless we, the many modellers from far and wide, who have each contributed some little to these notes, will still be at your shoulder, our thoughts and ideas crystallised into a book which helps to perpetuate that which is the noblest and most beautiful work of man, a ship.

St. John's Wood,   J. H. CRAINE
London, July, 1948.   (" JASON ").

Introduction

$\mathbf{A}$t a time when there is a marked upsurge of interest in the construction of ship models of all types, it is a pleasure to introduce this new edition of 'Ship Modelling Hints and Tips.'

Lt. Cdr J H Craine, R.N.R. (Ret'd) — 'Jason' — was known to modelmakers all over the world. For a period of more than thirty years he fostered and sustained a lasting interest in ship modelling through his writings in various magazines, by his assistance in the formation of ship model societies and lectures to them, and by an active participation, either as organiser or judge, at exhibitions of ship models.

These activities brought him into contact with a wide range of modelmakers, and if they benefited from his experience and advice, then he in turn amassed a very considerable knowledge of models and the people who made them, and of the many pitfalls awaiting the unwary.

In 1948 he put some of this accumulated experience and knowledge into a long-awaited book, under this apt title of 'Ship Modelling Hints and Tips.' No one book could hope to encompass so vast a subject as ship modelling, and the author made no attempt to describe the making of any particular model or type of ship. He confined himself to dealing with what he considered to be the most suitable method of approach to various aspects of the craft, and herein lies the value of the book.

Some may think, on reading through the chapter headings that, even so, he has omitted certain processes or references to prominent fittings. It must be appreciated that he has done this in order to concentrate upon the areas of model making which his many years of practical experience have shown to be those in which help and advice are most needed.

So there it is, chapter after chapter packed with useful, practical information, from choosing a subject for a model, to making the glass case for the finished article. With such a wealth of information at hand, it is invidious to select any particular chapters for special attention, but there are three which must be mentioned.

One of the most frequent problems confronting modellers is that of 'ropes'. The clear and concise explanations and illustrations in 'Ropes and how to make them', coupled with the details of the construction and operation of a simple rope-making machine, must go a long way towards solving this problem, and to assist in eliminating the faulty rigging which so often mars an otherwise perfect model.

Scenic models are undoubtedly one of the most attractive and worthwhile types of model to build. 'Jason' recognised this, and he also appreciated that many people hesitated over tackling a model of this type because of a lack of knowledge of seas, sails, and weather and of how to rig and position a model in relation to all three. So in 'Setting your model in a sea', not only are these matters explained, but there is also a detailed account of how seas (waves) are created, together with a most valuable table showing the appropriate sail to be carried by different types of craft under varying weather conditions.

Miniatures were another type of ship model in which he was particularly interested and the chapter on these contains information which will be found of use both by miniaturists and by others who, in the course of their work, have to produce very small fittings. The encouragement and help which he extended to those working in this field did much to advance the standard of craftsmanship now to be found on such models.

This is a book by a practical modelmaker — one who also had the unique advantage of a knowledge of ships and the sea gained from many years afloat, firstly as an apprentice in sailing ships, and finally as an officer in the Royal Navy. All those who now read this volume will find it, as did many others before them, to be of great assistance and help in their hobby of ship model making.

John L. Bowen
Upminster
1972

Contents

CHAPTER ONE

The fascination of modelling ships.

THE modelling of ships is a fascinating hobby because it has such a tremendously wide field of choice both geographically and chronologically. Its appeal to craftsmen and artist, youth and age, student and sage, rests on sure foundations ; for it is inexpensive, it is within the reach of all and, although within the reach of all, it still permits very broad standards of artistry, science, and craftsmanship.

Some years ago, while organising a huge shipping exhibition for the City of Liverpool, I decided upon a novel competition to popularise the ship model part of the exhibition. Competitors were invited to submit ship models wherein the materials had cost not more than three shillings. The results were amazing in ingenuity, craftsmanship, and popularity.

I feel sure that really fine models can be constructed for less than ten shillings. Unlike the model engineer, the requisite tools are few and comparatively inexpensive. Some friends of mine, good modellers they are, manage along with a favourite knife, spokeshave, small hacksaw and a few files (tiny ones) and some razor-blades. With these few things they consider themselves well equipped.

This, however, is not the real basis of ship modelling popularity. It lies rather in the wide range. Consider this. You have a choice, say, of making a ship of the Nile of 3,000 years ago, a Viking boat of 1,000 years ago, a Crusader's ship, a *Mayflower*, a Tyne collier brig of the 1820's, the first iron battleship, a crack Isle of Man cross-channel flyer, a humble " tramp " steamer, the Mississippi Show Boat, or the very latest liner. But that's not all. You can choose your field of craftsmanship. You may work in metal or wood as you please. You can choose as your medium something highly coloured, a " still life " type or an " action-scenic." Your work can literally be carried out on a corner of the kitchen table. A taxi driver I know did lots of his " fiddley-bits " while waiting for fares.

It is essentially a lone worker's hobby and more than in any other craftsmanship hobby each model bears the unmistakable stamp and personality of the modeller. Very often when going round some exhibition I could tell at a glance. " That's one of so-and-so's models." " Here's one by Zeroson ! "

Thermopylae   *Picture by I.W.Marsh*

Ship Modelling is democratic. I have seen a surgeon listening earnestly to a docker. They were a fine pair and the docker told me in his own language that the surgeons instrument cases were the Eldorado of ship modellers' tools.

CHAPTER TWO

There are so many from which to choose.

THE problem confronting the
modeller is " What ship shall I make ? " The number of different motives
which bewilder many modellers in their choice of a subject is really amazing.
Among sailors, love of ship and sentiment enter largely. Let me warn you,
however, that sailors are, as a rule, very, very indifferent modellers. They
usually rely upon a piece of dunnage wood, a few reels of cotton, some darning
needles, sail needles, and the dregs from the paint pots. The war-time sailor,
on the other hand, will probably tackle his first ship (dear to the eyes of any sailor
is his first ship) in which he served. The quality of his craftsmanship will
depend to some extent upon his civilian background, upon his aptitude and upon
his character. This latter is more important than it might at first seem.

In my opinion the very first requisite is some small bond of affection. You
must have some liking for the ship you would like to model. After all it *is*
a hobby, a labour of love. But this affection for some particular ship we must
examine more closely.

Now consider these words :—Personal, romance, adventure, hero-worship,
scholarship, curiosity, family connections, historical interest and so on.
Well, here are the explanations. Personal—because of service in the ship ;
romance—a friend of mine fashioned a ship because his parents first met each
other on board her ; adventure—consider the ships of Columbus, Drake or
Cook ; hero-worship—Scott or Shackleton is an answer here ; scholarship—
a young B.A. friend of mine fashioned " The Ship of the Odyssey " after
Homer's description, this forming his thesis for his degree ; but why continue ;
the reasons are legion. There is one inspiration which must not be overlooked,
the sight of an actual ship seen on holiday at the seaside, or perhaps, a glimpse
of her in some large seaport.

We will suppose, for example, you see a ship in some seaside place while on
holiday. She catches your eye. Instantly there grows in you a liking for her
and this fondness may be crystallised into a model, something concrete, and in
the many months' work there are perhaps moments you'd not change with
anyone.

Back to the harbour and the ship of your dreams. First take her name and

4

port of registry and then the owners' and builders' names and addresses. Go aboard her. Normally the crew are proud of their ship and will gladly talk about her. Ask permission to take snaps. Don't forget to take sketches and, on your sketches, insert some vital measurements. The crew will give you something of her history. It may be very good. I went aboard a tramp steamer once. I did not know previously who she was, but it was the Q5, or H.M.S. *Loderer*, our most famous mystery ship of the 1st World War, in which Captain Campbell won his Victoria Cross. You can't expect many ships like that, but do all you can on your holiday. The captain and owners may be able to lend you photographs of her. The builders if approached by a humble student, for that is what you are, will see that you will receive every reasonable assistance by the loan, gift or sale of lines and plans. Correspondence with the Captain or one of the officers will clear up forgotten odds and ends and details, which surprisingly mount up no matter how careful you may have been in your initial examination and measurements.

The above advice does not apply to all ships which " catch the eye." She may be a foreigner. Even so she may have been built in a British Yard. Don't forget to enquire if there are any sister ships and what differences, if any, there are between the several sister ships. Foreign shipowners are just as courteous as our own.

A small fishing vessel may not be quite so easy, but the procedure is generally the same unless she is old and small. Some vessels of that size never had lines and plans. She may be an open boat or half decked, or decked. You may have to take off the lines yourself. An interesting job this but within the reach of all persons of normal intelligence and some aptitude for surmounting minor difficulties.

There's still another kind of ship where some research may be necessary. Many of our coastal types are fast dying out. It may be your good fortune to find one of these. You'll certainly not recognise her for the queen she was once. She may be a shrimper with a 14 h.p. Kelvin motor. Her boiler (for shrimps) may be interesting to sightseers, but 50 years ago she might have been a smart Ramsgate smack with a main-mast and topmast three times the height of her present stumpy affair called a mast. Perhaps she has no mizzen at all. You'll have to be patient, noting the names of those who knew her in those far off days. Note well the names and addresses (and particularly the nicknames which are a valuable introduction). You'll be introduced to photographs, sketches and paintings both official and private. Above all never neglect the local library and the local Editors. Their help is usually invaluable. You may, too, be introduced to models, sailor-made models, coarse rigging with paint in quantity but not quality. You may be sure that the rigging, the standing and the running gear, is in its correct place and that there are no " Irish leads." The figure-head made from lead is now a mass of chemical salts. No matter ; here is

5

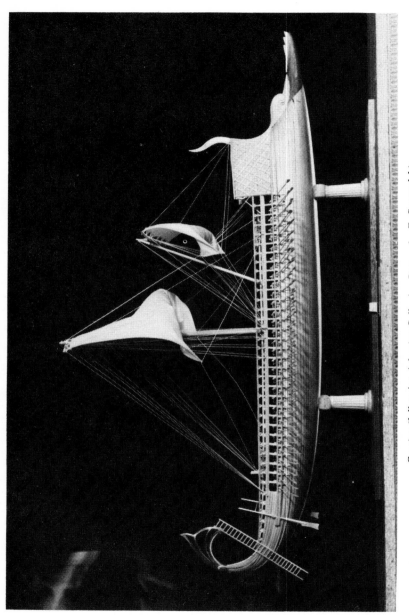

Grecian Galley (or Athenian Galley)   Picture by E. Capsoulakis

your queen in her home-made finery with each little piece in its correct place. Substitute correctly scaled rigging and sails, a boxwood figurehead, a coach-painter finish to the hull, which in a sailormade model usually is near to correct lines, and you will have a bygone queen again in something like her former majesty.

By now I imagine you'll not be short of ideas for a choice of ship, and having chosen her, your next work is to accumulate all the data necessary. It may be that you'll have some research work to do. Rest easy. It's very interesting, especially when it's difficult.

CHAPTER THREE

The ship of your choice.

RESEARCH is as wide as the world and as far as time. Don't be scared about research for *any model whatever* which happens to be your choice. Generally, it falls under three L's, the library, the locality, and luck, and strangely enough you'll be surprised how much luck comes your way—if you are very patient and persistent. Regard it as a contest, a game if you like. You'll enjoy it and you'll become an expert. You will also acquire that rare virtue, modesty. When one seeks knowledge one becomes aware of how little is the extent of one's knowledge.

You must make your librarian your friend, even the small country town librarian. He does not know very much about the ships of the 3rd and 4th Crusades, but he does know which path to take in order to find out. The encyclopaedias usually tell us a lot and often mention several authorities. These authorities in turn mention several other references, and so it goes on.

The Society for Nautical Research may be approached and in return *they* expect some of the fruits of your research. The South Kensington Science Museum has a fine library. So has the National Maritime Museum, at Greenwich. The Crusaders? Yes, of course. Didn't Richard Coeur de Lion have something to do with them? Yes, but which, the 1st Crusade or the 10th Crusade? Never lose sight of the fact that you want to model a ship of the 3rd Crusade. It may be that the ships were chartered from Venice by the English King, who made a start in some herring busses from Southampton. Soon you'll be in correspondence with Cinque Port people, or maybe some foreign museum, and one day you'll have two letters which state that (1) there were awnings over the stern castle ; (2) the usual colours for ship cloths were brick red and chrome yellow, because such and such materials were used in dyeing the cloth. Well ! That would be a good day's work. Perhaps you think this is an awful waste of time. Lots do, I agree. On the other hand, what's the hurry if you are happy in your hobby ? *You* must decide ! I have chosen here a particularly difficult subject for research. It may be that later someone else will make his model on *your research*. It may easily happen that research will become your hobby and a fascinating one it is. So much for the library, which is strongly recommended for *any* research on *any* ship of *any* period. Your librarian will

8

send out a call for any book you may want. I have had books from a dozen cities, including such places as Galway, Copenhagen, and Brussels. All dropped, as it were, on the mat by my armchair. The locality ! What better place to do research than on the actual site ? If you can visit the site, so much the better, but much can be done by correspondence. The starting point should be the town clerk, the chief librarian, or maybe, in some cases, the parish priest. In each case the questions are the same. *I seek information on the " NonSuch," about 1815, said to have been built and sailed from the port of Somewhere. Would you be good enough to send this letter on to the local antiquarian society, or to someone whom you think might help ?*

This method is usually very indirect in its results, because you'll probably get about five or six *further* references, maybe in various parts of the country.

You'll not neglect the newspapers, local, not national. Nevertheless, such papers as *The Times* and the cultural Sunday papers are helpful in genuine cases. I do advise, however, some restraint in approaching big papers until all else fails—which is hardly ever.

My own experience may be indicative. When I was organising the shipping exhibition in Liverpool, the thought came into my mind—What was the first steamer in Liverpool called ? Some weeks went by with unsatisfactory results. Then I used the press, local and national. Not only was the name of the first steamer established beyond doubt, but much other information came to hand, so much indeed, that a colleague of mine wrote a book on early steamships.

There are much better methods than the foregoing if the ship of your choice is a warship. The Admiralty are very helpful to modellers, especially if the approach is through a ship model society. Very often the Admiralty can supply lines, drafts, plans, etc., at a nominal cost. If blueprints have already been done for some previous enquirer, then the cost of copies is down to a few shillings. There is a valuable Admiralty library in Whitehall, and permission to use it is seldom withheld from any student of ships.

For merchant ships there is some difficulty up to the nineteenth century, especially in named ships, but on the other hand there are many cases of ships being hired or chartered by the Admiralty. Many of these transactions are recorded. Extensive refitting very often involved lines and plans being taken by the Admiralty. Thus we can, perhaps, arrive at, at least, a sister ship. The libraries of the bigger seaports very often have valuable information concerning local merchant ships. For example, in the Pottery Room of the Liverpool Museums there is a series of decorative tiles showing some very fine drawings and pictures of the cross-channel packets of 1770 and thereabouts. I know of no other information about this particular type of vessel and it is being recorded here so that it shall not be overlooked. I have not mentioned *Lloyd's Register*, which is a mine of information about merchant

9

ships. It includes the important measurements together with a multitude of other details. It is an " annual." Another useful annual is *Jane's Fighting Ships*, but, of course, this does not go so far back as *Lloyd's Register*. And what a wealth of ship knowledge is contained in the back files of our shipping newspapers, not to speak of such gold mines as the *Illustrated London News*. Here's nearly a century of pictorial history and usually very reliable too, for the sketches are naturally contemporary work by the best artists.

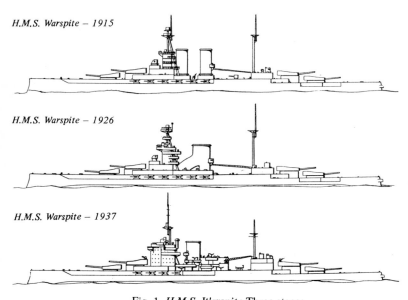

H.M.S. Warspite – 1915

H.M.S. Warspite – 1926

H.M.S. Warspite – 1937

Fig. 1. *H.M.S. Warspite* Three stages

Finally, beware of sailors. Bless them, they'll help you on ships of all ages if you let them, but again I say, be wary ; and this is the reason. I am a sailor myself. I served in a number of windjammers built from approximately 1880 to 1900. It would be quite safe to ask me about details of those particular ships, but none others, *unless* I have made a special study of them. Twenty years earlier the ships were composite or even wooden with double crews and all *pulley-hauley*. Brace winches were unknown. Halliard winches were perhaps dreamed of. There were no battens on the lower rigging. But perhaps you see what I'm driving at. Well this will ram it home chock-a-block. Get three navymen together, the first one who served in *Warspite* at Jutland, the second who served in her in say, 1927, and the third who served in her when she was ready to take on all bombers in 1941. (See Fig. 1.) Each of these three men would be quite unreliable in describing the *Warspite he did not know*, unless he had made a study of her. He might not be able to say how many funnels she had. Do not imagine that this is far fetched. I have proved it.

The Patent Office is worthy of scrutiny. There is a Patent Office Set of Records, concerning ships in the City of Liverpool, dating back about a century and a half.

One final paragraph about research. I have included a bibliography which I hope will be of use, and against each book there is noted the period or type dealt with. Many of these books are out of print and difficult to come by, but our mutual friend, the librarian, in such matters is a friend indeed. Luck is a fickle hussy. If she smiles, be grateful.

CHAPTER FOUR

Different kinds
& types of models.

$\mathbf{H}$AVING chosen your ship as a subject, how shall it be modelled ? Naturally, that is for you to decide, but on the other hand what types or kinds of models are usually made—and why ? Well here's a list of kinds of models with a brief why and wherefore.

THE BLOCK SILHOUETTE MODEL

This is a small affair the length of a cigar. It consists of horizontal layers of three-ply or other suitable thin wood. The layers are pinned or stuck together. Pins and cut lengths of wire form masts, derricks, guns, etc. The trick is to *leave off* the details. Tools—razor blades, wire pliers, and cutters. Scale : usually 100 ft. to 1 in.

THE MINIATURE MODEL

This is a cased and accurately made model usually in one of two well-defined classes, i.e., the " Still Life " type and the " Action " type. Whereas the block silhouette model may be made in 2½ hours, the miniature which is about the same size and scale may easily take up to 2½ years.

. My definition of a miniature model, for guidance only, is 9 in. limit to the overall length of the model, which is made to a scale limit not greater than 64 ft. to 1 in. unless of a small craft when 32 ft. to 1 in. would be allowed. In exceptional cases the scale limits might be increased still more. One of the finest models I have ever seen in the miniature class was that of a " service " whaler about the length of a cigarette and this gives a scale of 10 ft. to 1 in. This model showed planks, ribs, gratings, knees, rudder, yoke and lines, leathers (on the oars) rowlocks, painter and plug together with water breaker and dipper.

On the subject of miniatures, which is dealt with more fully later, I would only say now that it's not everyone's speciality. Very few indeed become really good miniaturists. Try a few little jobs with a watchmaker's glass, or it may be that your eyesight suits miniature work. Your trials will help you to decide if you can make miniatures with accuracy and with artistry.

THE SMALL SCENIC MODEL

This is by far the most popular type of model because of its very convenient size. Moreover, the glass case presents but few difficulties. Yet it is larger than the miniature and permits of much detail. The model is anything from 9 in. to 15 in. in length. At any time during construction the whole lot, materials and tools, may be kept in a small drawer or in a box on a shelf. When completed the small scenic model is easily packed, presents no difficulty in being displayed and has many of the virtues of the miniature and the exhibition models.

THE EXHIBITION OR STAND MODEL

As the name implies, this model is of the type and scale which allows full scope for detail, scale, and size. It is the kind usually shown in shipping galleries and museums and some modellers in this type have their work purchased by a museum. I should mention the warning that model making can never be regarded as anything else but a hobby. If, by the standard of your craftsmanship, you are commissioned to make a model, regard it as a form of honour but little else. The exhibition model requires a good airtight case of a size suitable for displaying the model. This case in itself is quite a job, but there is a special chapter on cases and transportation.

THE WORKING MODEL

A large number of people find much pleasure in showing the visible performance of their handicraft. The working model of a ship offers a wonderful opportunity for this. The words " free lance " will be met frequently in model boat circles. Thus a man may have a free lance design of engine in a hull modelled from a known prototype. Usually it is the other way about. The orthodox engine is fitted into a free lance hull, that is a hull that is like nothing on earth. Yet this is not to say that the hull is not suitable for the work required. During the last 15 or 20 years, however, the ship modellers have raised their standards considerably and the engineers have not been slow to notice this. The chapter on laminated and hollowed hulls will be of some interest to the beginner in working models, and there is no harm in suggesting that working models would not suffer in performance if made in the likeness of some definite prototype.

THE VOTIVE MODEL

In the Middle Ages it was customary for a crew, in gratitude for their safe return, to fashion a model of their ship and present it to their church, as an expression of thanks to God for their deliverance from the perils of the deep. The votive model has special qualities all its own. It is big, six to ten feet or more in length. It had to be, for it was slung aloft in the cathedral high above the congregation, for all to see. Because of this, two strong copper eyebolts were screwed or bolted through the deck, or rather hull, for they were usually

Gloria Brittannia or the Royal Prince *Picture by Isaac Sailmaker*

14

solid. There were no deck fittings and sometimes not even a deck. All sails were set and plenty of banners and bunting were flying. The guns and gun ports were prominent. Some of these are still aloft in Continental churches.

Recently this practice has been revived in this country. Models of ships from both Royal and Merchant Navies have been hung in our cathedrals in recent years.

THE DECORATIVE MODEL describes itself and examples may be seen in some of our large stores. A serious ship modeller would find it exceedingly difficult to make a decorative model in the popular style, yet I must confess many of our best modellers today have a decorative model hidden away somewhere. It might almost be described as the skeleton in the cupboard. There are other model types of course, but the foregoing are normally all that the modeller will need to know about.

The main part of any ship model, of course, is the hull itself, and this may be made in any one of several different types.

We will now consider some of the differing types of hulls.

CHAPTER FIVE

Various methods
of making the hull.

THE hull of your model is the
foundation upon which to erect the superstructures, the masts, rigging, and
sails. You may please yourself in the choice of material and even in the display
of craftsmanship. Briefly, a hull may be solid or hollow.

If solid, it may be in one piece or " bread and butter built," better understood by the novice as horizontal slabs glued together. The technical description of the latter method is lamination.

If hollow, the hull may still be carried out in several ways. The first and
obvious one is to hollow out the single block. Laminated hulls may also be
hollowed out and this is the method frequently followed by those who build
sailing model yachts. Each and every method so far mentioned has its advan-
tages and disadvantages, but these I will discuss in a moment.

The pinnacle of the ship modeller's hobby is the timbered and planked hull.
This, as the name implies, is the constructing of the hull of a wooden ship as
the shipwrights would do it, i.e., by creating the frames, knees, beams, etc.,
upon the keel and keelson and covering them with the " skin " of planks.

In addition to the foregoing there is ample scope for the metal worker.
He may fashion his hull from sheet metal in either one or several pieces. He

YOUNG AMERICA
American Clipper Ship of 1853

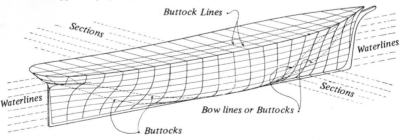

Fig. 2. Diagram showing lines of a ship

16

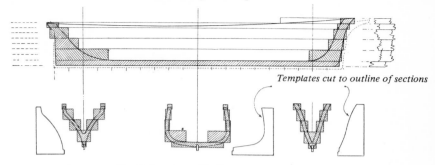

Templates cut to outline of sections

Fig. 3. Laminated hull construction

may emulate his brother craftsman in wood by fashioning the hull " in frame and plate," that is, in the same manner as the shipbuilder in iron and steel. Indeed, I have seen some wonderfully constructed hulls actually made from tin cans and the like.

It will be seen from what I have written here that these methods cover every requirement of expression in craftsmanship. Now let us examine each one in more detail for the why and the wherefore.

In deciding upon which method of hull construction to use you will be guided mainly by two considerations, viz. :—the scale or size of your model and your own ability and capacity. If you are a beginner, do not reach too far. Better to start something easy *and finish it,* than to embark on a project which overwhelms you, thereby undermining some foundation of your very character. It should not be necessary to mention this but my experience bids me do it.

The solid hull, for example, is obviously a method for very small models. A soft wood of excellent quality, well seasoned, is too expensive for large models. Above all it is wasteful.

The laminated hull has the merit of easier work and reduced cost. The thickness of the laminations should be made to suit the spacing of the water lines of the drawing (See Fig. 2 for diagram of these and the other " lines " of a ship.), and the utmost pains should be taken to ensure that the meeting surfaces are true. The longitudinal centre-line and the positions of the various stations or sections should be drawn on the upper and lower surfaces and edges of the laminations, and also the outline of the corresponding water line. Each layer should be cut out to the size of the larger water line which is usually that on the upper surface. If the hull has to be hollowed, the outline of the hollow should also be marked out on each side and the wood cut away to the smaller which is usually that on the lower surface. The diagram, Fig. 3, will make this clear. When all the laminations are cut out, they should be glued together in their correct relative positions as shown by the centre and section lines.

One of the modern waterproof marine glues should be used, either the casein glue or the resinous glues ; the latter are made to be used with different solvents so that they set slowly or quickly as desired.   With these waterproof glues, there is no need to use dowels or screws, so long as the contacting surfaces are true and the layers are kept under pressure until the adhesive is set.

The final shaping of the hull may now be carried out.   This consists largely of cutting away the projecting corners until the angle where the smaller layer meets the larger is just about to disappear.   These angles form a useful guide, but the chief guide should be the templates (see Fig. 3), which are cut out to the sections of the body plan, one for each section.   These should be shaped as shown on the diagram, Fig. 3.   They may be cut from Bristol board or even from old post cards ; thin celluloid or sheet metal also make excellent templates. See that each template and each pencil line on your block is plainly numbered or lettered.

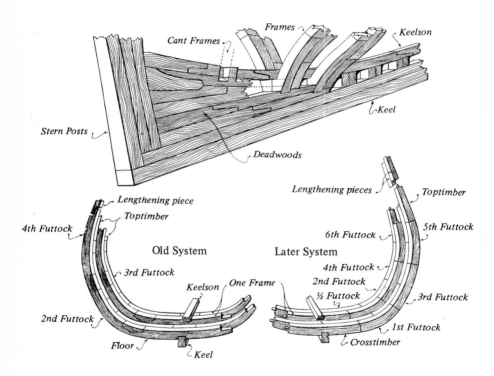

Fig. 4. Details of built-up model construction.

Midship section of *H.M.S. Rodney, 1823*

Perhaps you are one of those fortunate fellows who are miracle-men with an ordinary pocket-knife. It is worth finding out, but see that the knife is a good one with an easy, friendly grip in the fingers and hands. Above all, don't lose it, or lend it. A good pocket-knife or a pen-knife has a personality of its own which can be developed and built up in the years of usage.

Let us now consider the timbered and planked hull. I have to assume that you will be working to plans and detailed drawings of some sort. Select the

19

appropriate timber for its proper purpose. A timbered and planked model is, when all is said and done, merely a large number of small jobs. Some organisation is necessary. Some care and accuracy too are essential. Therefore do not be deterred by the maze of lines and " the bits and pieces." You will be at main deck level in a normal winter's spare time.

The novice should look at the sketch of a " frame " (see Fig. 4). It will be seen to be in two layers, each in several parts. Each part, except the " floor " across the keel, is called a futtock. For greater strength one layer of each frame has a cross timber or " floor." With each line of futtocks use a thin strip of beading lightly tied at the upper ends of the futtocks. This beading holds the whole in position and also provides a resting place and guide for the next set of futtocks. Your futtocks all being about the same size each alternate futtock overlaps its neighbour by half.

Frames may also be in one piece for smaller models.

Obviously, this handbook has not the space to develop timbering and planking. The purpose of this brief introduction is to show what kind of work is wanted and how very interesting a job it can be. The average full set of lines, plans and detailed drawings of a period ship are usually sufficient for the average modeller who has had a little experience in other types of models.

Approaching the framed and plated hull, i.e., metalwork instead of woodwork the same remarks apply. Strangely enough the names of frames, ribs, ties, carlings and a host of other strange names are found in both types of ship building.

CHAPTER SIX

Woods and other materials.

MANY of our younger readers have grown up in an age when fine timbers were unbuyable. Some remarks therefore concerning the qualities of the different kinds of woods may not be out of place.

Woods are broadly divided into two classes, viz. :—Soft woods and hard woods. If you can use a soft wood then do so by all means.

SOFT WOODS. First, let us look at the soft woods, bearing in mind our particular requirements. There are not so many of them, and by far the best is *Canadian yellow pine,* sometimes called Quebec yellow pine. It is a straight grained and very easily worked wood. It is suitable for almost any part of your model. At the moment of writing it is somewhat scarce, but is found in the most unexpected places. See my later references to marketing for your materials.

Siberian pine is a soft wood and it forms a substitute for yellow pine. It is grown in North Russia and should be fairly plentiful.

Columbian pine (or Douglas Fir) from the western slopes of the Rocky Mountains. Quite suitable for all purposes, especially hull and spars.

Whitewood and redwood. Whitewood is a larch and redwood is a fir. Both are largely used in joinery work. If you are reduced to these two then only the very best qualities are suitable for your use. Any inferior quality will lead to trouble.

HARDWOODS. It will be seen that some of the softwoods appear to be all-purpose woods. This is not quite true. Carving, for example, requires a particular kind of wood. Indeed, there are many items which require hardwoods. Here's a list of parts and items suitable to the medium of hardwoods of various kinds. All carvings and scroll work, keel, stem, stern, knees, frames, capstans, bitts, blocks, deadeyes, hearts, caps, wheel, etc.

Here are some details about hardwoods.

Ash (American and British). A white wood, very tough in texture with a long straight grain. Easily bent. *Suitable for ribs.*

Birch (Canadian and European) hard and heavy ; short grain and silky. Very liable to twist. Best left alone.

Teak (Burmese). Brown, very heavy, strong and tough, with a close even grain. Very durable. More suitable for ships than models. Suitable for spars because of its straight tough grain.

Alder (European). White. Mainly used in plywood.

Oak (American, Japanese and European). Of little use to the modeller but (with care in working) may be used for stem, stern, ribs, etc., for the open boat models, say 6 in. dinghies or 10 in. lifeboats (ship). Takes an excellent finish and pleasing appearance for small craft models. A straight grained English oak is suitable for most jobs, but is scarce.

Rock elm (Canadian and American). There are two distinct types (1) the *genuine rock elm* and the "*grey*" *elm*. The genuine rock elm is one of the best woods for a modeller. It is white with a long straight grain, tough and close in texture. This is the easiest timber to bend and is ideal for ribs, keels, stems, knees, etc. Very durable in water.

Mahogany (West African). Mild and straight grain. Good for many deck fittings. Central American is harder and has a straight grain. *Cuban* or *Spanish mahagany* is very hard and reddish in colour.

Poplar (American) otherwise *Canary Wood*. The sapwood is white and the heart is greenish yellow. It is of mild even grain, close textured, easily stained and takes a good polish. Because of its cheapness it could be used by the modeller instead of the more expensive hardwoods.

Boxwood (West Indian and Grecian). Very hard in texture and exceedingly close grained. Excellent for carving, blocks, figureheads, head scrolls, masthead caps, capstans and general deck fittings of all kinds. The sapwood is yellow and the heart is black.

Holly (British). White, very close grained and especially suitable for carving, small turned parts and blocks. Makes an excellent substitute for boxwood. Ideal for " turning " into guns.

Wych elm (British). White, very tough, long straight close textured grain, particularly suited for bending. It is somewhat wild so take care in working up.

Pearwood. Very expensive, but the first and best choice of wood for any modeller. The eighteenth century dockyard foreman used pearwood and boxwood for his models. When finished it gives a good clean sharp edge. Can be carved or worked into a splendid finish.

Hazel and pine. These two woods are of little use to the modeller because they are of exceedingly short grain and difficult to work. They split easily. Despite every precaution they will let you down in the end.

Here is a table which may prove useful for easy reference. It must not be regarded as the last word, but rather as a guide for beginners and inexperienced workers in wood.

Woods and Other Materials

MODEL PARTS AND THEIR MOST SUITABLE WOOD.

ALL GENERAL PURPOSES, except carving	Pearwood, sycamore, or Canadian yellow pine.
HULL carved from solid	(1) Columbian pine.
	(2) Siberian pine.
HULL Laminated (slabs)	Canadian yellow pine.
RIBS, KEEL, STEM and STERNPOSTS ..	(1) American or English elm.
	(2) Selected oak.
PLANKING	Mahogany or Canadian yellow pine. American rock elm.
SPARS	Canadian yellow pine, Siberian or Columbian pine, lancewood, straight teak.
GUNS (turned in lathe)	Boxwood or holly.
DECK HOUSES	Mahogany or Canadian yellow pine.
CAPSTANS, BLOCKS, FIGUREHEADS ..	Boxwood or holly.
SCROLLWORK AND CARVING ..	(1) Boxwood or holly.
	(2) Pearwood.
DECKING	Sycamore.
RIBS AND KNEES	Yellow pine may be used if good holding (for example, springy planks) is not required. American rock elm.
MASTHEAD, CAPS, DEADEYES, HEARTS ..	(1) Ebony or boxwood heart.
	(2) Elm.
	(3) Boxwood or holly.

See that your wood is well seasoned. A simple rule is *one inch of thickness requires one year of seasoning*. When you buy it ask how long it has been in stock.

If, of course, it is required for bending or shaping in any way the greener the better.

Here's a warning about steaming wood to make it bend easier. Bend it and keep it in shape until it is thoroughly dry, otherwise the seams and joins will gape wide open if it is allowed to dry in the fixed and final position.

Where to purchase fine timbers and woods is very often a problem. That is one of the benefits of membership of a society. Modellers in the course of years acquire bits and pieces of fine woods in excess of their own requirements.

Here are some tips which may prove useful.

The importance of yellow pine has already been demonstrated. Half a century ago only the very best Canadian yellow pine was used for the sides and bottoms of drawers in tallboys and chests of drawers. Consequently any

23

really dilapidated furniture probably has a few years' supply of yellow pine. Look out particularly for the backs of old wardrobes. Ebony and boxwood rulers can be purchased anywhere.

The junkiest of junk shops are the happy hunting grounds of the modeller in search of materials. Examine for example, some old dilapidated pictures. The glass will make your case. The oak frame is a godsend, but the biggest treasure is probably the thick back of yellow pine, very often flawless. It may be worth while clearing someone's attic of rubbish.

Demolition work and building estates yield riches. (a) Venetian blinds which normally are perfect pieces of wood and mostly yellow pine at that ; (b) the holly trees, and maybe pear trees too. In any event there's enough holly stalks a couple of inches thick at Christmas time to be found in any market place. The stall holder will be surprised at the offer of a shilling or so for some bits of unsaleable wood. Old fishing rods are good quality lancewood, as are also billiard cues (useful for spars).

Some factories receive machinery and parts from America and Canada. Sometimes they are packed in yellow pine cases. You'll have to pay for them, of course.

Shopfitters sometimes have second hand, but badly damaged, cases and shelving which have come from one of their contracts.

Usually most people are helpful to modellers in the supply of materials. The foregoing are only some ideas which might be followed with advantage.

Perhaps a few words about metals will not be out of place. Here we are all on much safer ground because a man who is willing to tackle metalwork must of necessity already have some knowledge of metals.

Anchors should never be made of lead. In a few years the lead is usually converted into chemical salts. The safest and best method is to file your anchors out of the solid piece of mild steel, unless, of course, a " trade " anchor suits your purpose.

Metal hulls. There is no reason at all why the hull should not be fashioned correctly out of metal frames and plates exactly in the same manner as is done in a shipyard. I have seen some very fine examples. Every effort should be made against insidious rust. Red oxide on the laps, butts and straps is essential, with an airtight case to finish.

Modellers in metal and indeed all ship modellers should avoid the use of too much brass. The use of brass in a model should not obtrude itself. If you like working in brass then use one of the many lacquers or enamels to take off the brightness. It may be that the use of a lacquer will also prevent in later years the appearance of verdigris or other chemical action. There are a number of bronzes and gunmetals which will probably serve the modeller in good stead. Silver tones itself down in a short space of time, so perhaps there is scope for the man who would like to indulge in silver plating.

Woods and Other Materials

I suppose, in spite of what I have said here, there will still be a tug of war between bitts made of wood, say boxwood or yellow pine, versus bitts made of metal, say " turned " from brass or iron or filed from the solid, either castings or solid.

The metal worker may, however, find some new delights in working in hard-woods and in experimenting in new materials. In this I must remind you to seek new materials on the junk stall. The old Victorian trinket boxes and the like, and other unwanted ornamental woodwork. There's a fine range of materials suitable for the modeller which comes under the heading of " Compo " (composition or modern plastic materials). These range from combs to corset-ribs and billiard balls.

Those who are unacquainted with electrical materials should collect a few ends of various kinds of " flex." Some of these " break down " into very many fine wires.

Entomological pins may be just what you are looking for. Let me explain. People who hunt butterflies and moths use a very thin and tough type of pin for holding them in the showcase. There's an old-established entomological firm in Welling, Kent, by the name of *Watkins and Doncaster. A box of assorted sizes of entomological pins will help in many parts of your model.
*Watkins and Doncaster Ltd., 110 Park View Road, Welling, Kent.

CHAPTER SEVEN
Making the different ropes.

ALL models require some form of cordage, and it follows that the cordage of a model should be reasonably correct in appearance and scale. This is particularly to be desired in the " period " ships of sail right up to the windjammers of the twentieth century. I have even seen an early nineteenth century ship model rigged with only two different sizes of cotton thread.

Even if you *must* use haberdashery threads, AT LEAST AVOID THE USE OF WHITE IN ANY SIZE. White thread stands out ; it looks big, and it certainly makes a model look top-heavy. Strangely enough, one of our foremost modellers, probably the greatest authority in the world on ship models and ship history in general, has given instructions that all signal halliards must be in white. Even though they are to scale, these signal halliards *do* stand out.

However, as a beginner you will be well advised to avoid white running and standing gear, except where it is correct, and that is in certain small yachts, mostly American, in which the prototypes are rigged with white cotton rope. The first thing to note is that ropes are measured, among sailors, by the circumference. The diameter then is approximately one-third. This rough rule is on the safe side. A golden axiom about rigging a model is, if in doubt about the scale or size of ropes, use the smaller size.

If you have to work out the size of rope to use on a certain part of your model, here's a rough and ready method of doing it. Using a walking stick or a pencil, lay your " rope " round and round as if binding the stick together. Let the " lays " of rope be as close together as possible and then measure carefully how many " lays " there are to an inch. This will give you the diameter or thickness of the rope expressed in a fraction of an inch. The circumference will be three times this diameter. If you are working to a scale $1/48$ (or $\frac{1}{4}$ in. to 1 ft.) and your three main size cordages are $3\frac{1}{4}$, $2\frac{1}{4}$ in. and 1 in. respectively, the following figures will be helpful.

$3\frac{1}{4}$ in. circumference is very nearly 1 in. diameter. The scale size of your $3\frac{1}{4}$ in. rope is therefore $1/48$ in. diameter. All your skeins of rope have a tag-label and probably your nearest one is $1/50$ in. thick., or in other words, you were able to squeeze 50 turns of rope alongside each other on a 1 in. length of stick.

In a short space of time you will become accustomed to judging scales approximately, but in starting a new model check your cordage scales very carefully.

Well! I was waiting for it! You'll have to make your own rope. Rope spinning is thousands of years old and, strangely enough, apart from varying materials, we have made very little progress except by adding a " heart."

Let us break down a rope. (See Fig. 5B.)

A rope may consist of three or more strands. A strand may consist of three or more rope yarns. If the rope is right handed then the strand will be left handed and *vice versa*. That is all the modeller needs to know of the structure.

The commonest material *was* hemp, a vegetable fibre, followed by manila in the late nineteenth century. Nowadays sisal is making some small head-way. Hemp was nearly always tarred. (*Stockholm tar, please, not coal tar.*) Consequently hempen rope is a very dark brown becoming slightly lighter with sun and salt. It is still used in a few places in windjammers, but has been replaced by wire in most parts of the ship, especially in standing gear. Manila is straw-bright in colour and because of its cheapness it ousted hemp from such jobs as running gear. Manila is not so durable as hemp ; nevertheless, it was extensively used towards the end of the nineteenth century. Wire rope came into general use in the latter half of the nineteenth century. Wire is of two kinds. The first is galvanised wire, stiff and hard, which is used chiefly for standing rigging such as shrouds, stays, and backstays. The second is flexible or working wire, which, as the name implies, is used for running gear such as halliards, braces, cargo runners, and mooring lines.

Let us break down a piece of wire rope. (See Fig. 5A.) Usually it consists of six strands laid round a soft heart of twisted jute, hemp, or tarred manila. Each strand consists of seven or more wire threads. These threads may, or may not, be laid on a heart, but mostly they are. The wire threads of the strand are usually laid " flat " i.e., they spiral round the " heart " but do not cross or twist round each other. The lie evenly alongside each other. The rope splice differs from a wire splice.

In larger scale models, especially period models, it may be necessary to worm, parcel, and serve some of the standing or running gear.

WORMING means using a suitably sized cord to fill up the spaces between the laid-up strands of rope (see Fig. 5, B and F). This worming is intended to convert the triangular section of a three-stranded rope to a more or less circular section in preparation for parcelling and serving.

PARCELLING is using strips of burlap, sacking, or canvas to cover the rope and its worming. The parcelling is the same width as the diameter of the rope being parcelled. It follows along the lay of the strands like bandaging a finger. Stockholm tar (not coal tar) is applied, as a preservative and air-tight seal.

SERVING is a continuous and close covering by a minor cord or twist such as spun yarn, houseline, marline, etc., round the already wormed and parcelled rope (see Fig. 5, C and D).   These covering turns are close together and the whole operation serves (a) to keep the rope watertight, (b) to act as a protection against chafing or rubbing by some adjacent part of the ship's equipment. I have a reason for explaining very fully *worming, parcelling* and *serving*.   It is important to show this covering and it can be done by either of two methods,

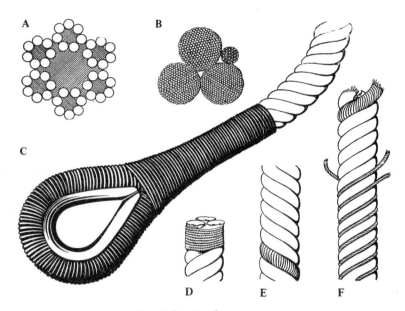

Fig. 5. Details of ropes.

viz :   carrying out the operation actually either in whole or in part, or by painting the part with several coats of black paint because it requires a number of coats to fill the spaces between the strands.   Be careful to ascertain what parts of the rigging have been " served " (includes also worming and parcelling) in your model.

So far as modern windjammers are concerned all wire eye-splices were served.   Most ships also had their shrouds served.   Some backstays were also done.   The wire tacks and sheets of the courses normally were served when made of wire (and I never saw any that were not of wire).   Footropes (with their stirrups) were always served, but sailormen disliked this because the condition of the wire inside was unknown. I saw three footropes part (break) with, luckily, only one man lost.

Once again I want to emphasise that coal-tar is never used in a ship, but only Stockholm tar. A limited use of Stockholm tar by the modeller is very strongly advocated. It preserves the rigging, it " sets " it, it colours it correctly (unless for manila which is very seldom tarred) and it has a pleasing and bracing smell of the sea. Moreover, it is less susceptible to dry and damp (stretch and shrink). Well, now let's make some rope in theory. Then perhaps we will make it actually.

We will make a three-stranded right-handed rope (see Fig. 5B and 5D) (5E is a left-handed rope) each strand consisting of seven threads or as I shall call them from now, yarns. I have made rope on board but I never had to spin yarn. Spinning a yarn is a tedious monotonous job and anyone who can tell a good story to ease the monotony is *spinning a good yarn*. Ropes are made in a " rope walk." Quite a long walk it is, too, in the old-fashioned places. Stretch out seven yarns making quite sure that all their tensions are equal. It is sufficient to see that they all hang evenly. Knot and make fast the " other " end. Now twist up " this " end between your finger and thumb as if you were winding up your clock with a right handed key. That's twisting your strand. Spun yarn is a twist, a strand only, and not a rope. Most kinds of string are twists but fishing lines and similar cords are " laid up " like a rope of three or more strands. As you've got to make your own rope you may as well know the basis of it all.

Let us start again to make another strand, but this time I want to introduce the spinning jenny (Fig. 6). The handle of the spinning jenny, by cogwheels, operates four hooks, rotating them round their own longitudinal axis.

By hooking your strand of seven yarns a twist can be imparted to the strand either right-handed or left-handed, as desired.

We will stretch out three lots of yarns, seven in each lot. See that the tensions are equal after having hooked each lot to an appropriate hook on the jenny, *and also hook the other end of each lot* to an appropriate hook on the sliding shoe B.

Perhaps you'd better take another look at the sketches of the jenny and the shoe. You'll see that each lot is clear of the others.

If you turn the handle left-handed (looking along the strands) the hooks will revolve right-handedly. The next step can only be found by experience but you should stop when each strand looks as if it would twist up into a nice rope. Now look at the sketches again. The shoe consists of five different hooks, four of them are fixed in that they do not revolve round their axes, but the fifth hook, C, in the centre is quite free to revolve round its axis, being centred within ball-bearings. Four fixed hooks are supplied because you *may* have to make a four stranded rope.

Unhook the three twisted strands and hook all three on the centre hook. Now carry on with the handle on the jenny in the same direction as before, i.e., left-handed or counter-clockwise; the strands will still twist up in the same manner as before. Now we introduce the " pear," D. It is a pear-shaped piece of wood fitted with a convenient stiff wire handle. There are four scores or grooves running from the " point " to the " bottom " of the " pear." Insert the pear, point towards the revolving hook of the shoe, so that the three strands lie in the three most convenient grooves of the " pear." Your assistant continues turning the handle left-handedly when, *hey presto!* the rope starts to form itself. Now some tips about the shoe. Use some pieces of lead or weights, E, on the shoe to exert some " pull." Many factors operate here. It may be on a polished floor or table or a mat or carpet. The stretch or if you like the " rope-walk " may be long or short. No hard and fast rule can be given here. There are resulting factors too. If the shoe is too heavy the rope will be very hard and tight. See the sketch for a guide as to what your rope should look like. The main guide is the spiral angle. Generally speaking, it will be advisable to lay your ropes rather loosely than tightly because of the final operation. A large amount of control over the quality of your rope will depend upon your use of the " pear " i.e., the speed at which you allow the rope to form up.

In due course, walking backwards, you and the " pear " arrive at the jenny. It is now advisable, using a cloth or chamois leather, to rub down the rope, but not too hard. When this is done turn the jenny handle *clockwise (right-handed)*, but not too much. Your rope now should have the same spiral angle as my sketch, and it is then finished.

It is assumed that you can make an eye splice, short splice and a back splice.
Frayed ends on ropes are distinctly untidy. For larger cordage whip the ends (i.e., a proper seizing) but it must be of the finest silk so that it looks like a whipping, see Fig. 5, D. A safe rule is that the width of your whipping should be about half the diameter of the rope. As there should be about eight or nine turns on the whipping it will have to be very fine stuff.

Here's a quicker and probably better way. Dip the end of your rope in a suitable glue or gum ; give it a twist or two between the finger and thumb. Then trim with scissors. It will set hard. This tip is essential for reeving off your rigging.

Use artificial silk for the main parts of your rigging. Black for shrouds, stays and backstays. Biscuit colour for the running rigging of modern wind-jammers, and darker, much darker, if your period is *before* the middle of the nineteenth century. Here's a specially useful tip. A very fine silk is to be found in the angler's kit—Pearsall's Gossamer fly silk. This can be obtained from Messrs. C. Farlow & Co., 56 Pall Mall, London, S.W.1. whilst Messrs. Down Bros. & Mayer and Phelps Ltd., Church Path, Mitcham, Surrey can supply surgical forceps and silk.

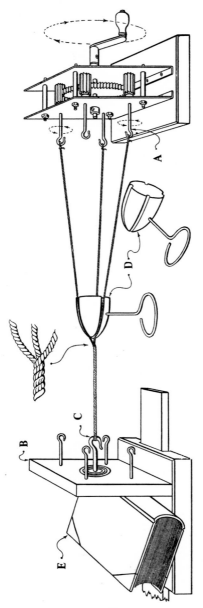

Fig. 6. A rope-spinning jenny.

This firm should also be able to supply surgical forceps of a special kind.   These forceps automatically remain closed and may be left hanging on the end of a rope.   A slight twist of the handles and they are open again.   I also recommend surgical silks for rigging, especially fine work, like miniatures. See the current issue of *The Lancet* for advertisements of surgical supplies.

CHAPTER EIGHT

What the early guns looked like.

MODELLERS in general usually slide over the question of guns as gracefully as possible either by leaving them out altogether or by the guess method. There is no reason why this should be so because there is ample information covering at least the eighteenth and nineteenth century periods. Perhaps, however, there is some excuse for the earlier times. Here then are some notes about the earlier guns up to Napoleonic times. It must be understood that these notes are for general guidance and any modeller tackling a " named " ship should refer to the several authorities mentioned by me and should note well the remarks on research.

Gunpowder made its appearance some time in the fourteenth century and guns certainly made their appearance in the following century. In 1474 in the reign of Edward IV an order was issued for the supply of bombards, cannons, and culverins. Modellers of this period should not overlook the additional interest given by fitting their ships with the normal catapult of the period. There were some wonderful mechanical contrivances for hurling a goodly sized stone in a well-aimed manner. I do not recollect ever having seen a model so fitted. Fig. 7A gives a sketch of an early English gun, of 1424. B shows an early Tudor gun. C is the celebrated Culverin 15 ft. long $5\frac{1}{4}$ in. bore firing a metal shot at 17 lb. D is the cannon of seven or cannon of battery and is over 12 ft. long. E is a stone shot cannon of 8 in. bore.; note reduced bore for the explosive. F shows the mortar. Particulars of guns C, D, E and F are taken from Prof. Michael Lewis's " Comparative Study of Armada Guns," published in *The Mariners Mirror*, Vol 28.

In Tudor times the use of guns on ships was well established, and even *in* ships too, for in 1501, Descharges, of Brest, pierced a ship's sides for gun ports. The names given to the guns were highly fanciful. Moreover, the performance was extremely varied. Modellers must note, however, that Tudor guns almost without exception, are characterised with the bands as shown in the several sketches. Indeed, these bands remained a feature long after the necessity for their retention.

In the middle of the seventeenth century there was a general codification of naval ordnance, and such names as the Murderers (of Henry VIII), Sparrows,

A

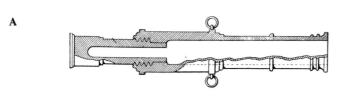

B

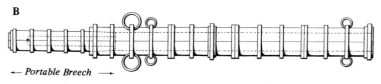

←— Portable Breech —→

C

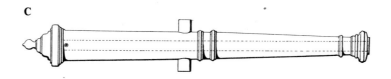

D

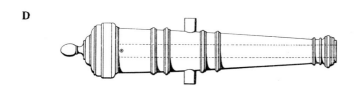

E

F

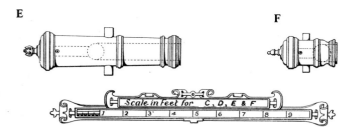

Scale in feet for   C , D , E & F

1   2   3'   4   5   6   7   8   9

Fig. 7. Early English guns

34

Curtalls, Serpentines, etc., disappeared.   Fig. 7 shows the relative sizes of the survivors and the following table gives some particulars.

SOME TUDOR GUNS
Their names, bore, weight of shot, together with reference to those guns which were later codified in Cromwellian times.

Name	Bore	Average Weight of shot	Average Length	Average Weight in lb.	Under Cromwell became codified as
Robinet	1″	½ lb.	—	330	
Sparrow	—	—	—	—	
Falconet	—	2 lb.	6′ 0″	400	
Falcon	2″	3 lb.	—	900	
Serpentine	See footnote	—	—	—	
Minion	3¼″	4 lb.	6′ 4″	1,200	
Saker	3½″	5½ lb.	8′ 0″	1,800	6 pounder
Demi-Culverin	4¼″	9½ lb.	9′ 2″	3,000	9 pounder
Basilisk	5″	15 lb.	12′ 0″	—	
Culverin	5¼″	17½ lb.	9′ 4″	4,000	18 pounder
Demi-Cannon	6¼″	32 lb.	10′ 3″	4,500	
Cannon Petro	6½″	24½ lb.	—	3,000	24 pounder
Cannon of 6	6″	30 lb.	—	6,000	
Cannon of 7	7″	50 lb.	—	7,000	
Cannon of 8	8″	40 lb.	8′ 6″	8,000	
Cannon Royal	8½″	60 lb.	11′ 0″		

The *Serpentine* in spite of the lack of details, is included herein because it is so often quoted by writers.   In the table it is in its relative position.   The *Sparrow* is another with few details but would probably lie between the *Robinet* and the *Falconet*. The first three or four guns were man-killers rather than ship-destroyers.   It is probable that many of the smaller guns such as the *Sparrow* and the *Serpentine* and others not mentioned here, were topped up with nails, pellets, and bits of chain for close fighting.   It was an early gun and not favoured by Elizabethan seamen.   The sizes of the guns varied extensively for a century and a half.   Even in late Tudor times the *Culverines* and the *Demi-Culverines* were longer in some cases by 4 or 5 ft. when they were used as bow-guns or chasers.   Some confusion is due to differing names (Flemish, French, Italian origins) for similar types and sizes of guns.

All the foregoing particulars are approximate to the average French type of gun.   The early Tudor guns were forged or cast in great variety.   See the illustrations, Fig. 7.   The student is referred to a series of articles by Professor Michael Lewis, in Vol. 28, *The Mariner's Mirror*, 1942. The foregoing table is mainly based on his excellent analysis.

This list does not pretend to include all known guns of Tudor and Stuart times, but rather a selection which includes those retained in the codification of 1650.   Many of those not included herein were very early guns, small and usually of a swivel type like the Rabinet or Robinet.   It is not clear what size the Murderers were.   They were made large at first and later were made smaller, even small enough to become swivel guns.   The smaller guns were sometimes made of brass.   *The Sovereign* (1488), originally was fitted with

35

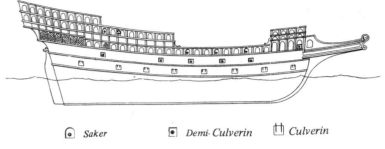

⬤ *Saker*   ⬛ *Demi-Culverin*   ⬒ *Culverin*

Fig. 8. *Warspite*, 1569

180 guns mostly small Serpentines. She was rebuilt in 1509 and mounted four curtalls, three demi-curtalls, three culverins, two falcons and eleven heavy iron guns. *The Warspite* (1569), offers a still better guide to the modeller of early Tudor ships, for not only are the size of the guns mentioned in writings of the period, but also their position in the ship.

Many examples of early guns are still to be seen in the Tower of London,

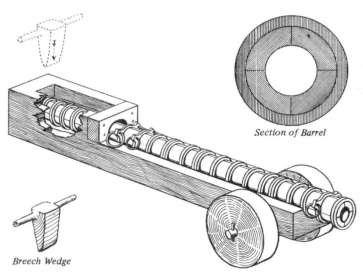

Section of Barrel

Breech Wedge

Fig. 9. Gun from the *Mary Rose, 1509*

36

and the National Maritime Museum, Greenwich. *Mons Meg*, in Edinburgh, is also worth looking at. There is some similarity between *Mons Meg* and a gun which was recovered from the wreck of the *Mary Rose*, of 1509, see Fig. 9. The gun was in two parts : the powder chamber was placed behind the breech. There were several chambers to each gun. While one was being fixed in position the others were being washed or taken below for charging again with gunpowder.

The carriage for the early Tudor guns is worth noting. There was a special " chamber-wedge " to take the recoil. (See Fig. 9.) It was obviously more economical to provide a new " chamber-wedge " than a new carriage.

Fig. 10. Trunnion gun, with cheeked carriage.

The shot was either stone or iron. There were rapid changes in the design of Tudor guns. At first the barrel of the gun consisted of four quadrantal pieces bound together by iron bands which are clearly shown in the *Mary Rose* gun (1509), Fig. 9.

We then began to cast our own guns and soon our gun-founders beat their teachers from the Low Countries. By the time of the Armada our seamen had had ample experience of guns and gunnery. Up to 1530 you are quite safe in using the 1509 type. They might be mixed from then onwards with late Tudor guns. From the Armada period onwards, all well-found ships would have the trunnion guns, i.e., the guns were mounted on a " cheeked " carriage which also had a form of elevating gear (see Fig. 10).

Note specially the change in the carriage during the first century and a half, and how it settled down in late Tudor days to a design that persisted until well into Victoria's reign.

In the time of Henry VIII, and the previous reign, Robinets, Falconets, Sparrows, and Serpentines were used in abundance, so that we read of *The Sovereign* (1488) having been fitted with 180 guns mostly Serpentines. Twenty years later she was rebuilt to carry and mount only a score of much larger guns.

Make a special note that gun ports were first pierced in ships' sides in about 1501.

Fig. 8 shows the arrangement and sizes of the guns on one side of the ship.

CHAPTER NINE

The story of anchors.

$\mathbf{I}$F you will look at sketches A and B on Fig. 11, you will see the very oldest of anchors which dates long before the start of history. *You are also looking at the very latest anchor.* Some fisherman at this moment, somewhere, is making a similar one as his own first anchor.

In the safe keeping of the National Maritime Museum, at Greenwich, there is a large case containing models of killicks. This name of killick goes back to the earliest times. It would seem to be almost as old as the boat itself. It means, very simply, an anchor. The general principle is the same throughout the whole world, and, one might add, throughout the ages. A stone, a piece of a tree branch and the rope. Through the ages each district has developed its own type, but all of them achieve their purpose ; namely, a weight plus a point or points to hold fast on the floor of the sea bed. If you should require further information about this, then write to the Director, National Maritime Museum, Greenwich.

Few modellers, however, will have any need for killicks but all, at some time or another, must display anchors. Many modellers have hazy ideas about anchors. It is quite simple to commit anachronisms. There are quite a number of anchor types, some of which have lasted a thousand years and others only a mere half century or even less. Each of these will help to " date " your model. The angle crown anchor for example, " dates " a model between 1702 and 1825. This applies to naval ships. One would be correct to ignore the angle crown anchor altogether in merchant ships. Indeed, the round crown anchor could be used on merchant ships right through fifteen or more centuries. Small naval vessels probably did not have angle crown anchors at any time.

I have thought it wise to include a sketch of an ordinary and conventional anchor showing the names of each part. (See Fig. 12A.) This may be found useful if you want to write about or discuss anchors.

Now let us look at some anchors.

Apart from the killick, which is a matter of wood and stone lashed together, we may roughly divide anchors as follows :

The Grecian mushroom anchor is dated about 400 B.C. This type of anchor still persists today in permanent moorings, such as those for lightships, buoys and river moorings. The ancient Greeks had a triangular eyebolt at the crown for " tripping " the anchor out of its bed. The Tuscan or early Roman anchor : the stock was usually made of antimony or a hard lead alloy, the arms, palms, crown and shank being of wood. Two holes pierced the stock. These were for the shank. There is a very fine example of a Roman stock in the British Museum dating to about the first century. It is made of antimony or a similar metal.

The sketch of the Tuscan anchor, see Fig. 11C, is based on the example found during the draining of Lake Nemi, near Rome. The finding of this

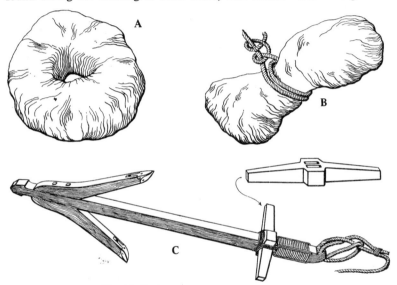

Fig. 11. Prehistoric and Roman anchors.

anchor cleared up many doubtful points. Note the curious cable bend or hitch which can best be described as a timber hitch with the end seized to the hauling part. The lashing of the cable is interesting ; note the stud arrangement in either side of the stock to protect the lashing from chafe. The shape of the crown and arms is still met with in native craft on the Mediterranean.

There is in existence an iron anchor of the Mediterranean type. It was found in Scandinavia, perfectly preserved, along with many other things. It probably was made about A.D. 700, and differs but very little from a modern anchor such as may be found in small coasting craft and even on big windjammers today, except that the stock is missing. There is no evidence to show what sort of a stock, if any, was used.

Admiralty pattern anchor

In early anchors, there was an eyebolt on the crown, and the ring was fixed. A modeller would be safe, in my opinion, in using the Mediterranean anchor with a simple wooden stock from the first century B.C.   The Tuscan anchor would also have a wooden shank.

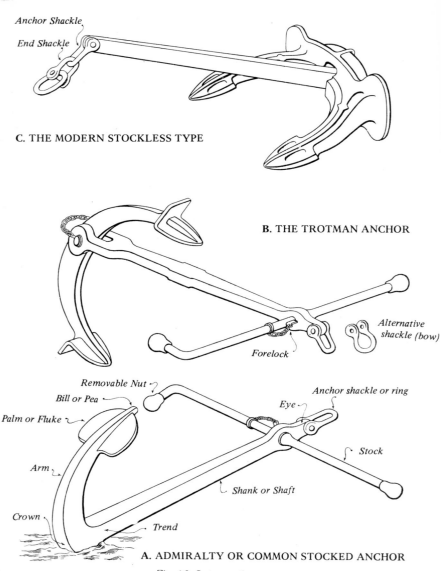

Anchor Shackle

End Shackle

C. THE MODERN STOCKLESS TYPE

B. THE TROTMAN ANCHOR

Alternative shackle (bow)

Forelock

Removable Nut

Bill or Pea

Palm or Fluke

Arm

Crown

Trend

Eye

Anchor shackle or ring

Stock

Shank or Shaft

A. ADMIRALTY OR COMMON STOCKED ANCHOR

Fig. 12. Later anchors

By the fourteenth century the anchor used on the English coast was the same as the anchors used in the nineteenth century. The seal of Poole shows one and the date is 1325. Probably the crusaders brought it back from the Mediterranean. Therefore the modeller should show the round crown anchor for all types of ships until the middle of the nineteenth century with one exception, viz., the larger naval ships from 1702 to 1825, for which he must use the angle crown anchor. In all these cases a wooden stock bound with iron hoops is proper, but it is probable that a very heavy one-piece stock was used in medieval times. The nineteenth century calls for special attention to anchors. In the 1820's, an enquiry into the too frequent loss of ships by anchor trouble led to the abolition of the anchor we know as the angle crown type for it was found that anchors broke off their arms at the joint with the crown. At the same time iron chain cables such as we know today were also introduced, but many merchant ships retained hempen cables for many years afterwards. *By the way, a fairly safe rule for the size of your hempen anchor cable* was *half-inch circumference for each foot of beam*, thus a ship with a beam of 40-ft. would have a cable 20 in. in circumference. A 28-ft. beam meant 14-in. cable. For diameter, of course, divide by three.

During the first half century of iron ships there were many attempts to invent new anchors and we modellers need only examine two of the new anchors, viz :—the Trotman and the Stockless anchors.

The Trotman anchor, see Fig. 12B, was a complete departure from the anchor which had been used for 2,000 years, and its use belongs to the period from the middle to nearly the end of the nineteenth century. It will be found on the early Atlantic liners, and perhaps on liners in general. The increasing size of steam vessels called for an anchor with greater holding power per unit of weight than was possessed by the existing types. Thus, we have among many others the Trotman anchor. It was a thing of many gadgets. *It had greater holding power undoubtedly.* It was easier to stow and secure on the fo'c'sle head of a liner. Nevertheless, sailors never trusted it. The arms, working on a pivot at the crown, did not inspire confidence. Before long it was ousted by the stockless anchor which was a complete break with anchor design as man knew it throughout the ages. (See Fig. 12c.) This design permitted the anchor to be hove up right into the hawsepipe and automatically to stow itself in a matter of seconds.

The writer, when in windjammers, frequently had as long as eight hours' work for more than half the crew in fishing, catting, bedding and securing the bower anchors. Frequently this had to be done in something of a sea which did not make the operation less dangerous. Now we have reached the day of the 20-ton anchor which can be stowed securely to face an Atlantic gale in a matter of twenty seconds by a supervising officer, and engineer and the carpenter.

The design for the stockless anchor is simple. The crown and the two flukes are in one piece. The shank is fitted into the crown so that the tips of the flukes are free to move through an arc of ninety degrees. Both flukes are flat in the same plane and the crown is pivoted to the shank. Indeed, the shank acts as the limit stop for the arc of movement.

Now for some tips on making anchors. There is only one satisfactory way. Make your own anchor unless you can purchase one to the correct scale. *Avoid lead.* As a youngster, I used lead for my mast head-caps and anchors. They turned into beautiful lead salts in a couple of years or so. File anchors out of a solid piece of iron. It's not such a long job. Use boxwood for the wooden stocks. Be guided by naval sizes if you are working on a merchant ship prior to the nineteenth century. For the nineteenth century and after you'll find that there are a number of excellent seamanship books. The Board of Trade has been the governing body for anchors during the past century. The Stationery Office has publications which cover the sizes and tests for anchors for the last half century or so.

CABLES AND HITCHES. I have referred to the size of the hempen cable (which should be very dark brown) and that is half-inch of circumference for each foot of beam of the ship.

Chain cables were introduced about the middle eighteen twenties, but were by no means in universal use for some time afterwards.★ Studs were added much later. The stud of a cable is the piece of iron in the middle of the link. (See Fig. 13.) ★Consult Board of Trade rules for this. The windlass for chain cables is different from the windlass for hempen cables.

The question of the cable hitch has, in the past, generated much heat. Modellers, therefore, should pay special attention to the following remarks of mine which I think will help them to overcome this difficulty. There are two methods of attaching the hempen or rope cable to the ring of the anchor. One is called the " cable hitch " and the other the " fisherman's bend " or " yachtsman's bend ". The former, see Fig. 14B, is for big ships with large cables in deep and good anchorages. The cable in this case is a four-stranded (left-handed) cable-laid rope. The latter, see A, Fig. 14, is for very early ships, and in more recent times for smaller vessels in estuaries usually with a muddy and slimy bottom. The loops shown in the drawings are, of course, drawn tight in the model.

You can safely use a " fisherman's bend " up to 1540 on any ship.

Sometime in the reign of Elizabeth with the heavier cables required by the increasing size of ships using deep water, better holding ground, and, perhaps, the need for speed in attaching cable to ring, the simple " cable hitch " was

Now the department of Trade and Industry.

★Laing's, the Sunderland shipbuilders, launched the *Kent,* 195 tons, in 1814. She was fitted with chain cables. Note : the size of a chain cable is indicated by the diameter of the iron from which the link is formed.

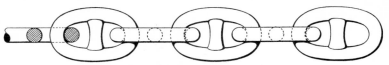

Fig. 13. Studded anchor chain

brought into use for the bigger ships. It is no joke trying to tie complicated knots in a 20-in. rope. The " cable hitch " was by no means in general use until the Restoration period, or later, and even then only in bigger ships.

Unless, therefore, you have quite definite evidence to the contrary, use the " fisherman's bend " in all ships except First Rates up to 1680. The use of the "cable hitch " in all big ships would not be questioned seriously after, say, 1610, or thereabouts. From 1740 onwards the " cable hitch " may be extended to frigates and continued thereon into the nineteenth century. The Royal Navy and the Merchant Service frequently use differing terms for the same object, e.g. the "cable hitch" of the West Indiamen is the "cable clench" of the King's Ship.

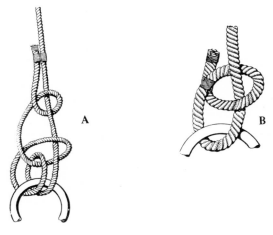

Fig. 14. Attachment of cable to anchors

CHAPTER TEN
How to make
gratings.

WHEN a few modellers get to-
gether for discussion someone is sure to ask the question : How do you make
your gratings ?

I cannot give you *Punch's* answer. Gratings *must* be supplied for a very
wide range of models over a period of at least three centuries, and so far as I
know the methods of construction have remained unchanged for centuries.
The main purpose of a grating is to supply a covering for a deck opening which
admits light and air and, at the same time, provides a safe working deck for the
crew.

In the sketches (Fig. 15), it will be seen that the prototype is a simple joiner's
job. A joiner would evolve some sort of jig or gadget to make his work easier.

If the modeller is expecting me to describe some wonderful trick of turning
out gratings he will be disappointed. There is no short cut. Indeed, by the
very nature of the subject, great care must be taken in making your model
gratings if they are to look neat, regular, and shipshape. Fig. 15A shows the
ship-carpenter's method and Fig. 15B a suggestion for easier work in modelling
which will still give a presentable grating.

You will be well advised to use boxwood as your material. A couple of
boxwood rulers will probably supply the full needs of a model. The second
tip is to make yourself a jig on the same style as a mitre board. (See Fig. 15C.)
Needless to say, it must be made with great care. This must be cut for your
particular scale.

Now I must discuss the sizes of the prototype. I have never seen the holes
in a grating larger than 2 in. square sides. For a large scale grating such as
the jig in the sketch would be used for, the sawcuts, although very narrow in
themselves, must be so measured that the space left by the part which is cut
away is equal to the part left behind. Even in a very thin saw-blade this must
not be ignored. Do not forget that your sawcuts are not all the same depth.

Hold your strips in the jig with a piece of flat wood and a clamp at each end
with the jig in the vice.

In such examples the lower battens are usually 2 to 2½-in. thick, while those
on top will be 1-in. to 1½-in. thick. A grating for a small hatchway does not

46

need such heavy wood, but of course, for wide expanses the grating must be of a stout construction.

I have seen gratings with a ½-in. mesh, for example, in a windjammer on either side of the wheel for the helmsman to stand on, not because it was thought necessary to keep his feet dry, but so that he could be raised up to get a better leverage on the 6-ft. wheel. Behind the helmsman there would be a grating on either side of the wheel-box which covers the ironwork of the steering mechanism. These two gratings were seats 6 ft. or more in length, but although of a large mesh, say 1½-in., yet of very light construction.

There was usually another grating used as a mat, at the entrance to the companionway leading to the saloon below. This grating saved wearing a hole in the deck; also it was lighter than a solid piece of wood and was less liable to rot the deck below.

I have mentioned these few examples of gratings to show their many uses on shipboard apart from the obvious ones of hatch-covers. In the absence of any detailed measurements, do not be tempted to make your gratings over-large.

If you have to show gratings on a very small scale, excellent effects may be obtained by using a very fine open texture chiffon or suitable material. Some

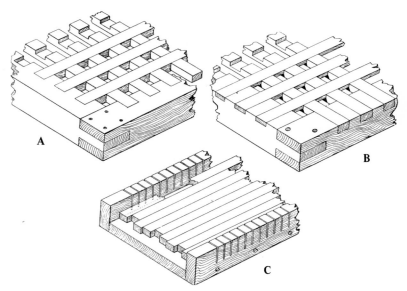

Fig. 15. Gratings with a simple jig.

47

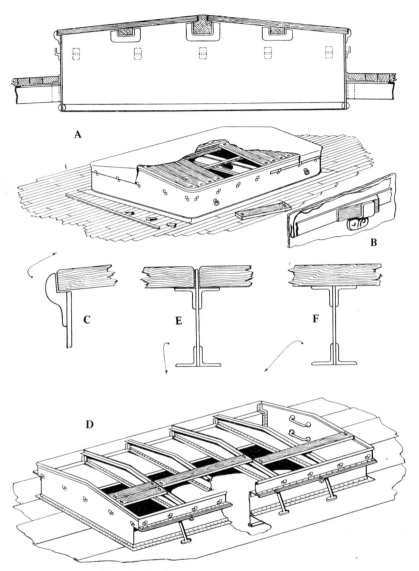

Fig. 16. Hatchways, sailing and steamships.

face powder compactums (your sister will explain) have an openwork sieve affair which may be just the scale grating you are looking for.

If you'd like to experiment in materials examine the yard-broom bristles. If your sawing and filing is above average I can also recommend the use of bones. Horse bones are best and the best part is the shin bone. You'll find it worth the examination. The older the animal the harder the bone.

If you're a beginner, however, stick to holly or boxwood.

Your final rubbing should be in fine pumice stone powder on a very flat surface.

Finish with methylated spirits and gold size. (See " Finishing.")

Hatchways, see Fig. 16, when large, are divided by thwartship beams, each end resting in special sockets in the hatch coamings. In addition there are " fore and afters " along the centre also resting in sockets. The whole of these works, i.e., the hatch coamings, the " fore and afters " and the beams are " rabbeted " in order to take the hatch-boards or hatch-covers or hatch-gratings.

Tanker hatchways are usually very small unless the ship is used also for carrying other cargoes. The hatchways on large liners are usually small affairs, 20-ft. long or less, frequently the cover is an iron plate hinged at one end. Fig. 16A shows the hatchway for a typical windjammer. The fore and afters shown in the cross section rest at each end in projecting sockets riveted to the coaming, the hatch-boards which are 2 in. thick, rest one end on the fore and after, and the other end on the coaming, as at C ; the side fore and afters supply additional support. Tramps and cargo liners usually have big hatchways similar to that shown in Fig. 16D. This shows a typical hatchway, but as details vary considerably, the actual ship being modelled should be consulted in each case. In the hatchway illustrated, the hatch-boards run in a fore and aft direction, the crosspieces being removable. The crosspieces are built up of plate and angle-iron, the section being as shown at E for the cross-members at the division of the hatch-boards, and as shown at F where they are used to support the middle of the hatch-boards. All hatches are covered and secured for sea by several tarpaulins, the edges of which are held by flat iron bars approximately 2 in. by $\frac{1}{2}$-in. resting in brackets which are 18-24-in. apart. Wooden wedges jam the flat bars against the tarpaulins, thus wedging them securely against the hatch coamings ; this is shown at B.

CHAPTER ELEVEN

Helpful hints on earlier davits.

AS in most other items of ship equipment some care must be exercised in displaying the davits proper to the ship and to the time.

In dealing with " period " ships a reference to a contemporary painting or sketch may prove exceedingly helpful.

Here's a list of davit types :
(1) Poles with sheaves of brass.
(2) Bent or angled wooden baulk davits.
(3) Straight wooden baulk davits (temporary).   Navy.
(4)   „   „   „   „   (permanent).   Navy.
(5) Stepped iron bow-shaped radially operated davits.
(6) Quadrantal foot davit.
(7) Gravity davits.

It will be found that these types overlap each other and in some cases it is a very big overlap.   Some of the davits too are temporary affairs and when they have served their purpose are stowed below or out of sight.

Davits were first mentioned, as far as I can trace, in the stores list of one of the Royal ships in 1543.   They were used for anchors, not boats.   At the same time there is also mention of " poles with sheaves of brass for the hoisting in of boats."

It is these poles which are the starting point for our davits as we know them today.   For a thousand years seamen have taken in their boats by any convenient yardarms and tackles, and still do so today if there is time for hoisting a boat in or out in a leisurely fashion.

Should sudden disaster come upon the ship there were plenty of gratings, kegs, casks, and the boats on deck, together with sundry spars and booms, for men to cling to in the water.   Now the anchors presented a different problem.   There were no yardarms over the bow or fo'c'sle head and anchors were needed *before* disaster.   Consequently, we can understand why a davit was of great help in anchor work.   This davit appears to be something like the fixed wooden davit of the sailing whaler.   It is still to be seen today, and is known as the cat-head.

Unless you have definite evidence, do not attempt to show a davit before the eighteenth century, and then only in the sailing whalers. Here you can show two pairs of davits, or even three pairs of davits on each side. The eighteenth century whaling men were the smartest men in sea history at getting their boats away. The davits were wooden, 8 in. or 10 in. square section, or more (see Fig. 17B). There was a curve or bend at the upper end, just as in a " knee timber." Sometimes these wooden davits were straight and inclined outboard. In the whalers the davits were usually fixed.

During the eighteenth century in ships of the Navy the " poles with sheave

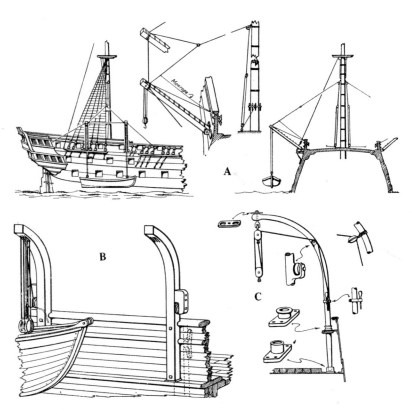

Fig. 17. Davits (old type).

or brass " became quite stout baulks of timber. It was not until the conclusion of the Napoleonic Wars that they became a permanent fixture.

The davits now became stout timbers 10 in. or 12 in. square in section. The heel was rounded and fitted as a hinge on the outside of the hull (see Fig. 17A.) I am indebted to Admiral G. A. Ballard for an excellent description of this type of davit. He was shipmates with them and has much to say in praise of them and also of enlightenment. I can do no better than quote him.

" *When I went to sea seventy years ago nearly every wooden ship, from frigates upwards, carried a pair of wooden davits on each quarter for hoisting in her cutters.*" Many of the earlier iron vessels were also fitted with the two pairs of wooden davits.

" *Wooden davits as I knew them were stout oak baulks of square section, hinged with a rounded butt about half-way down the ship's side. The davit was fitted with double sheaves for the boat falls at the head and carrying an iron crown band with eyes for the topping lift and the guys. They were kept up by a chain topping lift, rigged span fashion with two tails at its outboard end, one for each davit.*"

s.s. Great Western, 1837   *Picture by Iris McNarry*

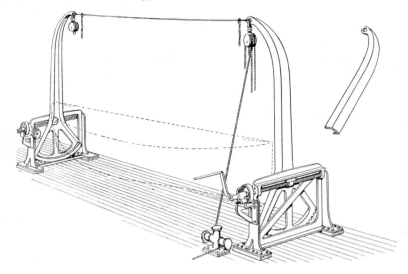

Fig. 18. Davits (quadrantol arm type)

There were two positions for the davits (a) outboard position, making an angle of about 40 deg. with the water, and (b) " topped up " position almost vertical. The boats were quite well stowed and secure in either position. No gripping spar was necessary.

Note on the sketches the battens on the davit, and the chain topping lift with a tackle hooked on ready for topping up the davits. There was also a main rope for each davit.

There is one type of davit I must not forget. They were fixed and built in the ship and were in use in the seventeenth century, and, perhaps, earlier. I refer to the davits over the stern or counter. They were a special feature of eighteenth century ships and during the Napoleonic Wars these were the only type of davits depicted on paintings, sketches and the contemporary models. The stern davits are still in use on all small craft around the European coasts.

All through the middle of the nineteenth century the wooden davit and the iron radial davit were frequently found side by side on the ships of the Royal Navy, but not on the merchant ships. There are many reasons why the wooden davit was retained in the Navy, but this is not important for the ship modeller.

Iron radial davits (see Fig. 17C) were fitted on the famous Transatlantic Steamer *Sirius* (a merchant ship), in 1838. Also about this time they appeared

53

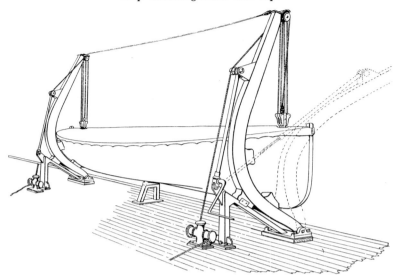

Fig. 19. Davits (telescopic screw type)

in Royal Navy ships. The famous prints of the contest between the *Alecto* and the *Rattler* (ordered by the Admiralty to test screw versus paddle) show iron davits on one of these vessels. Should anyone, therefore, contemplate making a model of a naval vessel belonging to the first three-quarters of the nineteenth century he would be well advised to enquire about the type of davits whether iron radial, wooden (straight) and in the case of the latter whether fixed or occasional. By occasional I mean " unrigged and stored away after use."

I have an excellent print (drawn in 1853) of H.M.S. *Queen* (120 guns) just before she went to the Crimea. She is on the port tack under plain sail and listing to the breeze. A boat is hanging in straight wooden davits on the port side of the poop. The remarkable thing about this is that the davits have been lowered down almost to the horizontal position. Yet this appears to be seamanlike because, being a 3-decker, there's a considerable distance to go to the water and the ship has a list. It is not usual to launch a boat with the ship under weigh. Also, make a special note, she is wearing a Red Ensign.

The iron radial davits of more than a century ago appear to differ very little from those of today. There is the bulb head with its snap headed male member arrangement for the upper block of the boat fall. There is a " lead " sheave on the " shoulder." There is the belaying pin at waist height.

54

By the way, just in case your information does not indicate the actual diameter of the iron davit, here is a rough guide to prevent gross errors :

For small accommodation ladders 1½-in. to 2-in. diameter.

For gigs and small lifeboats, say 20-25 ft. long, 3 in. to 4 in. diameter, double blocks, 2¼ in. rope fall.

For large type lifeboats 4 in. to 5 in. diameter, treble blocks ; 3¼ in. rope fall.

The largest type on big liners at the end of the nineteenth century, 6 in., but not over 8 in. diameter, treble blocks; 3¾ in. rope fall.

The iron radial davit was commonly fitted on steam vessels all through the nineteenth century and it is as well to describe it in more detail. It could be fitted either inboard or outboard. Towards the heel it tapered slightly almost to half the general diameter. The heel fitted into an iron socket from 1 in. to 2 in. deep, which was usually in the scupper or at main deck level when fitted outboard on the hull. The davit, when inboard, passed through the pinrail (main rail) and, of course, was free to move radially on its heel.

A thin wire stay joins the pair of davit heads. This wire stay is hooked into a " butterfly " or " double eye " which is free to swivel no matter how each davit is moved. On the other eye there is a guy which leads to the forward or after positions ; the purpose of the guys being to maintain the davits in a

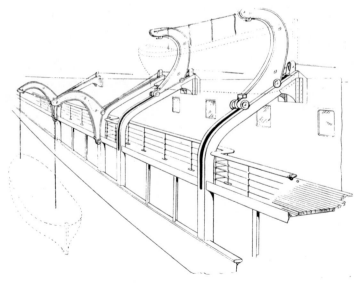

Fig. 20. Davits (gravity type)

" still " position when lowering the boat and also to operate the davits radially.

In the beginning of this century various attempts were made to improve lifeboat launching operation. These attempts were hastened by such disasters as in the sinking of the *Titanic* and *Empress of Ireland*, which had incurred serious loss of life.

The problems were " boats for all " and easier manipulation and launching of boats.

The results were " nests of boats " later replaced by larger boats with motor power. Flexible wire falls were introduced, eliminating the treble block rope falls and most important of all was the introduction of the quadrantal arm type, the telescopic screw type, and the gravity type launching gear. (See Figs. 18, 19 and 20, which are based on material supplied by Messrs. Welin-Maclachlan Davits Ltd.) In the quadrantal arm type, Fig. 18, by turning a handle a worm thread operates a female block which is attached to the arm. The arm has a quadrantal foot resting on a similarly " toothed " tramway. The arm in the " out " position overhangs well clear of the side. There is a simple brake releasing gear. If you have to show these on your model in some detail, purchase a current issue of a shipping magazine, or, perhaps better, still, write to the actual makers. They are usually willing to help. *Brown's* or *Reed's Nautical Almanac* (annuals) are usually chock-a-block with illustrated adverts useful to the ship modeller.

In Fig. 19 the dotted lines show the telescopic screw extended and the davit moved to the position for lowering the boats.

The sketch of the gravity type patent davits showing both positions, see Fig. 20, may be sufficiently detailed to help you in your model.

It is very important that you should ascertain what type of davits were in use for your particular model, and the date is very important. Many ships have had extensive alterations from time to time in their careers and this may have involved a change in davits.

CHAPTER TWELVE
Portholes, gun-
ports, scuttles, etc.

MODELLERS will find many snags
in the matter of holes in the hull of a ship, even as late as the end of the nineteenth
century. Generally speaking, ship modellers have neglected almost all of the
nineteenth century ships apart from the windjammers, 1880-1900, and a few
of the Clipper ships, 1850-1880. The really rich harvest of the early steamers
and the Atlantic liners up to the 80's offer a wonderful field to the modeller
in the picturesque and even the beautiful.

The main purpose of this chapter is to deal with portholes (Merchant Navy),
scuttles and side scuttles (Royal Navy), the gunports, the windows, and the bulls-
eyes. Some knowledge of these will help to fill in gaps in the lines, drafts,
and plans which may come your way.

It is a strange fact that the modern naval architect should devote so much
of his skill to the pursuit of piercing—with safety, of course—as many holes
as possible in a ship, whereas his pre-historic ancestor was fearful of exceeding
the original hole which he so laboriously dug out of a selected tree-trunk.

Who made the first hole ? Was it for light or fight ? A window, a peep-
hole, or a place to shoot an arrow through ? Noah, nearly 5,000 years ago,
spent 120 (or was it 12 ?) years in building the Ark and placed one window
therein, a window of onyx, or perhaps, jade. Glass, in an opalescent form,
was known to the Egyptians of that time, but not in a form suitable for a window.
Britain's oldest boat, which is almost as old as Noah's Ark, had a row of holes
along the gunwale. They may have been for peepholes, for arrows, or for
holding a wash strake. I refer to the *Brigg Boat* (Lincolnshire), of about 1,000
B.C. Three thousand years ago the Phoenicians had oar holes in the hulls
of their biremes and triremes. Grecian galleys of 600 B.C. had windows in the
after " house " at the stern.

There is plenty of evidence to prove the existence of windows in the deckhouses of St. Paul's ship (A.D. 60). Dr. Jules Sotas describes her as of about
400 tons displacement, a typical Roman merchantman, with a house 20 ft.
long on the foredeck, fitted with windows and .doors.

Probably the first windows in English ships were copied from Mediterranean
ships at the time of the Crusades. Those deckhouses had no roof and the
windows were open.

About 1400 a small church at the mouth of the River Seine, in France, had a stained glass window fitted showing a ship of the period with several round holes in the stern of the ship. No guns were shown, but in the succeeding part of the century there were many gunports in ships. These gunports were of all kinds and shapes ; square, oblong, round, *fleur-de-lis*, ace of clubs, etc. There were no port lids such as we know them, and these gunports were mostly in the upper works, fore and after castles, etc. Guns and gunpowder were coming into use, but bows and arrows, slings, catapults, and other engines of war, were still being used. In Maso Finiguerra's etching *The Embarkation of Pope Pius II for the Basle Assembly*, there is, in the port side of one of the ships, an arched doorway. This was definitely an innovation. We may be sure that sooner or later a resourceful seaman would poke a gun through such a hole. The artist was a Florentine, born 1426. Another artist (Flemish), whose main work was done between 1460 and 1480, was known as W. A. He shows in one of his paintings a stern gallery with at least one doorway and perhaps five doorways. This painting may be dated 1470. All the foregoing leads us to the gunports proper. The date for these is 1485, but they were located in the poops and fo'c'sles only ; the piercing of gunports in the main hull took place in 1501, and is attributed to the French.

At the same time vessels were being fitted with very large windows to the poop quarters with an outside gallery or " walk " on the three sides ; port, starboard and aft.

It is at this stage in maritime history that the ship modeller should exercise care in his ports, scuttles, and windows. And this period includes those hardy annuals, the *Santa Maria* and the *Golden Hind*. Both the *Santa Maria* (1492) and the *Nao Victoria* (1515) (first round the world) had rather large windows in the poop, and glass, suitable for glazing, had not then been in use for long. These, of course, were leaded windows. Henry VIII built his *Great Harry* (1514) to impress the French, and her three-decker poop had many windows and gunports which were needed for the 184 pieces of ordnance.

In 1545 the *Marie Rose* foundered because the water rushed in through her ports which were only 16 in. above the water. It may be said that the fifteenth century abounded in ports of all kinds, sizes, and shapes, as if each ship and each ship designer were trying out ideas without arriving at any fixed result. This went on into the sixteenth century when such happenings as the foundering of the *Marie Rose* caused a halt.

Gunports were important to Hawkins, the principal ship designer to the Elizabethan seamen. By piercing safe gunports in the hull, guns were kept low in the ship, upperworks and tophamper were jettisoned and, most important of all, in the case of the *Ark Royal*, they were fitted with *hinged and exterior* lids. These gunport lids existed right up to the nineteenth century. Figs. 21A, 21B and 21D. P. & O. *Coromandel*, built 1885, had them. Tudors and Stuarts

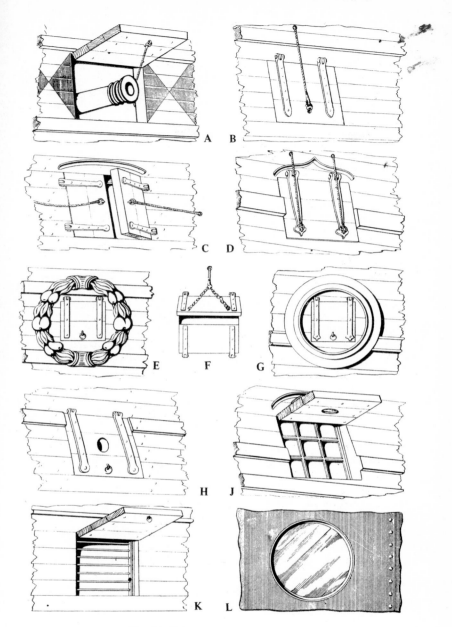

Fig. 21. Gunports, various types

59

did not bother greatly about light or ventilation. Bad weather meant closed gun ports.

Note here that round holed gunports survived for lighter guns and were found in the square tuck of the stern and forward in the fo'c'sle. The gunports of Stuart ships were usually surrounded by carved ornament and were known as wreathed ports. (See Fig. 21E and 21G.) Wreathed ports were in use up to the eighteenth century. Some were divided horizontally, as at Fig. 21F.

MODELLERS SHOULD NOTE SPECIALLY that the line of the gunports did not follow the sheer of the ship in Tudor times, Stuart times, or even right up to 1750. The decks were without sheer and were broken up into a number of levels convenient for working the guns and for the accommodation. A line of gunports parallel with the sheer would be wrong before 1750. The early eighteenth century also had a few *vertical* lids to the gunports, i.e., in two pieces and hinged on either side. (See Fig. 21C.) However, this did not become general. The stern windows were richly decorated in the seventeenth and eighteenth centuries. There is an excellent book on old ships' sterns and figureheads, by Carr-Laughton. Generally speaking there is plenty of information about the stern in the average set of drawings.

In 1740 on Anson's famous voyage round the world, he ordered six scuttles (round holes) *to be cut in each ship where it would least weaken the ship.* This was in urgent response to the strong representations of the captains in the squadron about the sickly condition of the crews. 1,500 men out of 2,000 were lost on the voyage, mainly by disease.

The round holes referred to were plugged up in extremely bad weather with a plug. Captain Cook, less than 40 years later, probably was responsible for the Admiralty order to cut a scuttle in every other gun-port. A year later it was in *every* gunport (see Fig. 21H). An inside cover was provided which hinged laterally. These scuttles, or rather side scuttles, were about 6 in. in diameter. Strangely enough they are seldom shown in models.

In 1780 glass windows were used in merchant ships inside the gunport lid so that light was possible in spite of a spray (see Fig. 21J). The same ships also used hinged port lids for the stern windows. Forty years later, in 1821, the steamship *Victory*, London to Margate, also had nine windows aside and four astern. From now onwards the development is rapid.

So we have the port lid, the port lid with a hole, the port lid with a window behind, and then the port lid with a bull's-eye glass inserted in addition to the window behind the lid.

We shall see how this bull's-eye glass later became hinged finally leading to the abolition of the gunport lid.

A patent was taken out in 1807 for the bull's-eye glass already referred to. This invention was adopted for use in the Navy two years later. The bull's-eyes were known as " illuminators." It was comparatively easy to fit these illuminators as the holes had already been cut in the gunport lids.

For the next half century the usual practice was to fit a bull's-eye in the gunport lid. The lid could be hinged upwards to show the window behind (see Fig. 21J).

The merchant ship *Liverpool* (1838) shows 16 bull's-eyes on each side in the gunport lids on her maiden voyage across the Atlantic. Yet the *Durango*, sailing ship, built for the Australian emigrant trade in 1841, was fitted with gunports, but there were no bull's-eyes in the lids nor windows behind the lids— just an iron grille (see Fig. 21K). In the 'forties and 'fifties large rectangular windows were being fitted (glass 1 in. thick) the patented invention of Thomas Gray. The modern porthole (see Fig. 21L), a circular glass in a hinged metal frame on a rubber seating first made its appearance in 1863. Progress has been made by increasing its size and lowering its position in the hull.

A few sailing ships had portholes fitted in the " half-round " of the poop. I have seen at least two ships like this. A deadlight is an iron-hinged cover which is fitted over the porthole. Some windjammers were fitted with these along the 'tweendecks presumably for use in fine weather. No glass was fitted in these. Glass ports are usually fitted with a deadlight behind for safety as well as for " darkening ship."

The foregoing should help a modeller of period ships to avoid anachronisms, for few sets of drawings—if contemporary—show all such details. If not contemporary, any such details should be carefully checked.

CHAPTER THIRTEEN

Early flags and house flags.

THE late W. G. Perrin, in his book *British Flags*, provides a wealth of data for the flags of ships from the Shetlands to Shat El Arab, and from the Euxine shores to the Azores. I only propose to deal very briefly with some of the more important aspects of the subject.

Our first national flag, the St. George's Cross, remains with us today. It might have been used as far back as 1400 *as a streamer only* (see Fig. 22D.) There were other decorations such as standards which later gave way to banners. Long tails made the banners into streamers. Coats-of-Arms were also displayed. In early Tudor times enormous streamers would hang from truck to water. At this time too the ensign was introduced and was displayed on the poop. The usual form was a St. George's Cross in the canton with a horizontally striped flag of several colours. The first of the Tudor ensigns is probably one in Henry VIII's reign, a small St. George's Cross in the canton on a flag with seven horizontal stripes, four green and three white (see Fig. 22K). Subsequent variations in the stripes were, red, white and blue, white and blue, red and white, etc. The stripes were increased from seven to nine (Fig. 22, M, N, P, Q) and subsequently to thirteen (Fig. 23C). It is interesting to note that the thirteen stripes, red and white, of the United States flag came from these striped Tudor and Jacobean flags via the flag of the Honourable East India Company. Some of the East Indiamen ships were present at the Boston "tea party."

In 1606 came the union with Scotland and the superimposition of St. George's Cross upon the white St. Andrew's Cross. A quarter of a century later, the Navy was given the sole right to use this union flag, and merchant ships went back to St. George's Cross in the main. The jackstaff was introduced at this time. Stripes on the poop ensigns had been abolished a few years before with the exception of the Honourable East India Company, who retained their ensign till 1824. Scotland broke with England on the execution of Charles I, and the union flag was in abeyance until 1707.

Red, white and blue ensigns had been in use at sea by the Navy from the early part of the seventeenth century for tactical reasons only.

In 1674 the red ensign (with the correct and appropriate canton) was ordered for the merchantmen. A modeller is therefore safe in using a red ensign from this year onwards for any British ship. A St. George's Cross at the fore was also permissible, but no Jack. *Warning.* See that your red ensign has the correct union flag in the canton.

By the way, Tudor flags may safely be tied with robands. Jacobean flags in the Navy were on halliards *hoisted from the top* and not from the deck. Merchantmen may still have continued with robands. In a period of ten years, 1700-1710, there were no less than four different white ensigns. If your ship comes in this period it's worth consulting Perrin in the local library.

In early Tudor days, the nationality of a ship was indicated by flags at the fore and main. Personal striped ensigns came into use on the poop in about 1580. In 1674 merchant ships were ordered to replace all poop ensigns, striped or otherwise, with the red ensign (B, Fig. 23.) The Levant Company was granted a flag in 1581 " to be set in the tops of ships." This flag was Queen Elizabeth's royal standard, the arms of England, superimposed on a St. George's Cross. This was used until 1605, and rightly, I think, this could be described as the first house flag. The Honourable East India Company used a striped ensign on the poop, this had the proper Union Flag in the canton right up to 1824, when it was abolished as an ensign but continued in use by the company until the middle of the nineteenth century. Similarly, the Hudson's Bay Company flew the red ensign from 1670. This had the Union flag in the canton ; it was probably used originally on the poop, but was later flown at the main. In the 1820's, house flags began to be worn generally at the main. Fig. 23A shows the house flag of the Guinea Company (from Charles II to 1752). C shows the flag of the Honourable East India Company as it was in 1824, originally there was no St. George's Cross. D shows the flag of the Hudson's Bay Company ; this company is still permitted by warrant to wear its flag at the main in certain latitudes and longitudes, i.e., the Canadian high seas. Another type of flag commonly used in merchant ships was the master's or owner's coat-of-arms, this was flown at the main, the arms of the port of registry being flown at the fore.

Very large flags were used in the seventeenth and eighteenth centuries, especially in battle.

SIZES. As a general guide to the size of flags, the following notes may be useful :

Streamers of *circa* 1293 were about 30 yards long by 2 yards wide at the base. Ensigns of *circa* 1623 measured 9 yards by $5\frac{1}{2}$ yards, while the flags on the mast head measured 12 yards by $7\frac{1}{3}$ yards.

The early eighteenth century ensigns measured up to 17 yards long by $9\frac{1}{3}$ yards deep.

The largest modern ensign is 11 yards long.

The largest modern Union flag is 9 yards long.

Before leaving this subject there are two important warnings.
In 1801 the present Union flag (not Union Jack, by the way), was introduced. Modellers almost without exception use at least one representation of the Union flag. For goodness' sake make sure that it is correctly drawn. On Fig. 23 is a scale drawing for your guidance. Here's a tip, use rice paper or cigarette paper and mapping pens with artists' colours or inks. For bigger models experiment with note papers, the thin India paper type. You can curl paper by rubbing a knife edge horizontally across the surface.

With reference to Fig. 22, A shows the flag nailed to the pole, or mast, which was usual in the Middle Ages. B shows the flag attached to a tube of stout material such as buckram, the tube being slipped over the pole or mast head. Later, flags were secured to the mast by robands, as shown at C. In the seventeenth and eighteenth centuries, flags were attached to ropes and then made fast to halliards, the halliards being belayed at the tops. D shows a streamer of Tudor and Stuart times, this is a forerunner of the pennant of modern times. E is the banner or banneret used on early galleons. A short pennant as at F is used as one of the signalling flags. G is the broad pennant, H the burgee, J is the present day " flag." The sketches F, G, H, and J show the various methods of attaching the flag to the halliards, as practised at the present time.

The oldest flag of all is probably the Dannebrog, about 1100. This is the forerunner of the present National Flag of Denmark.

Early English ship flags, apart from the banners, bannerets, etc.,

of knights	1250
Probable early use of St. George's Cross	1300
Probable early use of St. Andrew's Cross .:	1400
First Ensigns on poop	1520
Union flag (St. George and St. Andrew)	1606
First St. George streamer, with red, white and blue streamer ..	1623
Red, white or blue flags for squadrons	1630
Union Jack and jackstaff	1630
Abolition of horizontally striped ensigns. (Except Hon. E. I. Co.)	1630
On the execution of Charles I, we went back to pre-Union flags	1649
Parliament Jack (naval)	1649
Red Ensign (St. George Cross) for merchantmen	1674
Red Ensign (Union with Scotland) for merchantmen ..	1707
Union with Ireland (present Union flag)	1801

HOUSE FLAGS

In the early Victorian times a big business was usually the property of one family by which it had been built up. It was quite fashionable to refer to the business as " The House of Brown " or " The House of Robinson." There

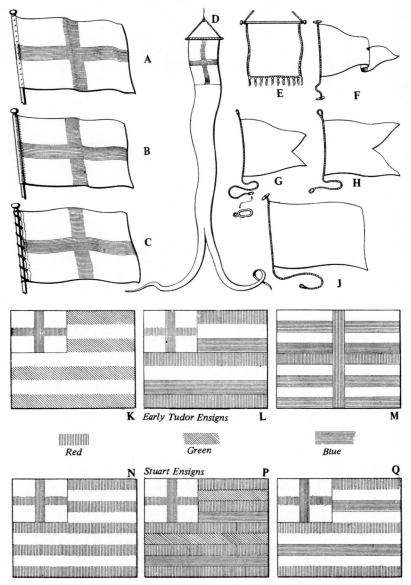

Fig. 22. Early flags *The colour key does not refer to figures A.B.C. and D which, of course, are red crosses on white ground.*

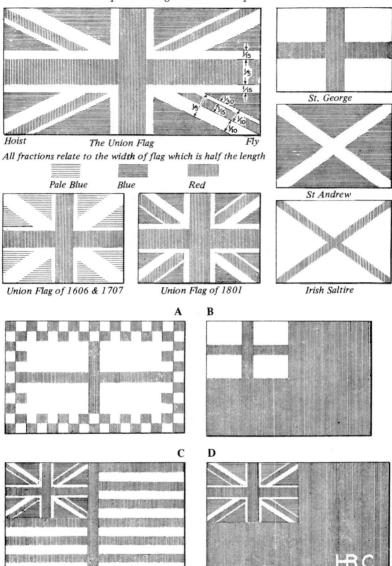

Fig. 23. The Union flag and House flag

was justifiable pride in " The House " by the family, the staff and servants and by the customers. This pride and zeal was something very real and alive It found many visible and outward signs. One of these was the house flag. It was in the shipping houses that the house flag flourished. The Merseyside navies of Bates, Holt, Brocklebank, Hoult, MacIver, Elder, Rae, Allen, Cunard, and a hundred others were " houses " just as equally famous names in Scotland and on the Thames were also " houses." There were literally thousands of house flags, and it is impossible to show or describe them here. It would be invidious to select a dozen or a score or a hundred. What I shall do is to offer a few notes upon the unusual types, indicate some avenues of research and issue the warning that you should check your results very carefully.

Generally the house flag is flown at the main. At least one company flies its house flag at the fore. Some houses, for a variety of reasons, have two flags. For example, the Cunard-White Star Line has the double flag, Cunard over White Star flags. The Ellerman Fleet consisted of some half a dozen companies and the plain little pennant with the letters J.R.E. surmounted many a famous house flag in token that these famous companies had passed under the control of John Robert Ellerman.

I can say that many a house flag was revered in foreign ports more than many national flags. Still, we are ship modellers and sentiment must be left to the old " shellbacks." Our job is truthful portrayal, artistic if possible, but always truthful.

Now for your hunting grounds. The chapter on research will help a lot. If you can establish the name of the company owning the ship at the appropriate time your search is much easier. We are dealing, of course, here with a hypothetical case of a vessel wrecked half a century ago. Another important line of search is her trade. Demerara ? A letter there to three persons, viz., the secretary of the Chamber of Commerce, the manager of the local bank (name supplied by your own banker), and the Harbour Master. These are only suggestions. The best place is the local seaport library. Do not forget the wonderful little magazine *Sea Breezes*, James Street, Liverpool. The results here are sometimes truly amazing. There are two shipping papers, *Lloyds List* and the *Journal of Commerce*. The Port of London Authority, the Mersey Docks and Harbour Board and similar bodies are helpful. They possess very old records. Finally, the*Board of Trade officials may help. There is a very fine collection of house flag prints to be seen in the Poplar Public Library.

When communicating with anyone concerning your query, send all your collected information about the ship to enable them to make an easier search.

There were printed from time to time large sheets showing the house flags (with funnels) of various companies. Many of these sheets were published by the *Journal of Commerce*, James Street, Liverpool. The few remaining are guarded carefully in libraries. So don't forget your own librarian. There were also some publications on house flags by Messrs. Brown, Son and Ferguson Ltd., of Darnley Street, Glasgow.

Before I leave the subject of flags on your model, I must give you a note or two on how to display them on a mast or staff. It is important to have the flag right up to the masthead. In large-scale work, flags are sometimes made of silk, and roped. Make quite sure the toggle or clip is close to the upper corner of the flag, otherwise it might be mistaken for a flag at half mast. In showing a flag at half mast, one-quarter of the distance down is quite sufficient.

One other matter—the wind. Make quite sure the direction of the flags (*and* the halliards) conforms to that of the wind. Try also to give your flags the folds and quivers according to the strength of the wind. Most ships use small flags for bad weather and large flags for fine weather. Dip your halliards in a solution of gum (weak, of course). Thus you can " set " the halliards in any curve and direction you desire.

Now the department of Trade and Industry.

CHAPTER FOURTEEN

Flags on your model.

WARS between nations have been fought because of flags on ships. The correct flags on a model, therefore, are no less important than the other main items in the make-up of the ship. The choice of the flags is a vexed question because there are so many flags and even the same flag displayed in different parts of the vessel means something different in each place. Do not therefore treat the matter of flags lightly.

Let us examine this question. First : The display of flags may be merely decorative or to convey a definite message.

Second : There are a number of different sets of flags and one set must not be mixed with another.

Third : These different sets of flags may have replaced other sets of flags because of changing conditions, requirements, or of their obsolescence.

Fourth : There is a very large number of national flags. Each nation, for example, may have a dozen or more state flags of various kinds.

Fifth : There are private flags, including house flags.

Therefore it follows that we must know the date of our model if we wish to display the flags correctly. The reason for the date is to determine which set of flags to use. A naval vessel, for communication, may use either the private national set of flags or the international code appropriate to the period. A naval vessel could not and would not use the naval code when communicating with foreign warships or any merchant vessel. The use of signal flags to convey messages from ship to ship or ship to shore dates back only two centuries, and one and a half centuries cover the general wide use of codes or sets of flags. It is, however, quite easy to blunder seriously on state or private flags as far back as the time of the Crusades. The modern code used is the International Code of Signals, and consists of 24 flags and 2 burgees (pennants with two tails) one for each of the letters of the alphabet. There are also ten numeral pennants for the digits. There is also an answering pennant for easier and quicker signalling. Finally, there are three extra pennants known as first, second, and third substitutes. These latter enable a letter or a number to be repeated three times in the same hoist. The use of the special answering pennant (red and white vertical stripes) indicates that the International Code is being used. This modern international code replaced, in 1935, a code which was then over 30 years old, which in turn had replaced the code used since the middle of the nineteenth century. These codes consist of two main parts ; first, a set of varicoloured flags each one being allotted a letter or a digit. Second : A code or key-book giving meanings for each possible combination of two, three, or four flags. This code is truly international for a ship of any nationality can communicate with a ship of any other nationality. It is, of course, impossible for anyone to look at a hoist (i.e., one, two, three, or four flags hoisted as a group one above the other) and say quite offhand what it means. It is possible to memorise the meaning of a single flag signal and also many of the two-flag hoists, while quite a few of the three-flag hoists are known to the signallers by reason of common usage. For example, " What ship is that ? " " Bon voyage ! " " What is my longitude ? " But the issue of a new code book as in 1934 changes most of the meanings again.

There are certain groups of signals however which are recognised by all signallers and lots of seamen too, and it is just as well that the modeller should know this. Here are some examples of what I mean. Four flag hoists having G or H flag uppermost indicates the name of a British ship. This is the commonest hoist on our ships. Certain initial letters indicate different subjects. For example, a glance at the hoist will tell at once whether is is a geographical place name ; a time signal (in hours, minutes and seconds) ; a latitude, a longitude ; money, weights and measures, from a sen to a cental or a quart to a quintal ; a medical term, and a host of other grouped subjects. This shows the modeller that he may display flags on his model but to do so correctly he should show the flags of the correct code, and also the group subject of the hoists should be generally familiar to him. He should avoid showing 1935 flags on the *James Baines* running the Easting down in 1855 or thereabouts. She probably used the *Marryat Code of Signals for Merchant Ships*. If you live in or near a seaport the coastguards will help in questions of the modern code, and perhaps also, the 1901 code ; so will the Lloyd's Agent. There is probably a Nautical School which will help. A phone message to a signal station will clear up your problem in a few minutes. By the way, don't forget that all these people are busy people and a letter will be appreciated, because it gives them more time to look up things, and, moreover, they can choose a less busy time to reply. On the question of naval codes, write to the Secretary of the Admiralty (through your ship model society) stating exactly your requirements, being careful to state name of ship, date, place, etc. *It is assumed that you will not ask about the current naval code.* I am referring particularly to historical craft, say, up to the first world war. There are quite a number of cheap handbooks about the International Code on the market. For obsolete codes I refer you to the usual sources of information as in research.

List of obsolete codes of signal flags which at one time were in common use :

1817-1880. Captain Marryat's Code of Signals for the Merchant Service.
1857. First International Code of Signals.
1901. New International Code of Signals.
1905. Pilot Jack Table and Signal Manual.
1934. Latest International Code of Signals.

In addition to the above, numerous small but private codes existed in each trading company. *The Brethren* had their own signals, so had the *Buccaneers*. *The Privateersmen* from the great ports such as Liverpool and Bristol had codes of their own, for the privateers were smart ships and well-manned. An efficient

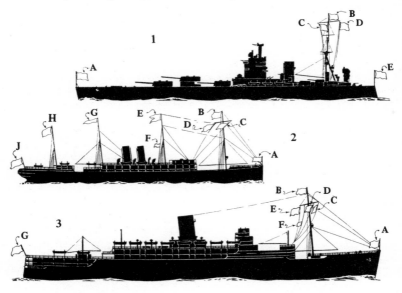

Fig. 24. The position of flags on various types of ship

signalling system was but a part of their smartness. However, the modeller need not bother about such small codes but he *should* take heed of the nineteenth century codes beginning with Marryat's Code. There is a possible exception and that is in the case of the *Honourable East India Company's Ships* of about two centuries' service, terminating in the early part of the nineteenth century.

Now for the state flags or the national flags. For an easy start I'll deal with a four-masted liner at the Landing Stage, Liverpool, say in the year 1910. She is British. She is registered in Liverpool. Let us discuss her flags because later we have to condense the subject for and on a *one-masted liner*.

Right up in the stem there is a tiny flagstaff. On it, rightly or wrongly, flies the white bordered pilot jack, A, Fig. 24.2   This is a Union flag having a 1/5 white surround.   During the nineteenth century this pilot jack was frequently used as a flag indicating "*I want a pilot.*" It was the official signal and it was flown on the foremast.   " Jack " is said to come from Jacques (James) at the time of the union between England and Scotland in 1603. This was the beginning of our Union flag. It has been argued that the merchantman is not entitled to fly a *Jack*. However, many thousands of ships in the Merchant Navy have done so for generations.   Moreover prior to the first world war, a special code was instituted called the Pilot Jack Code, which was a quick and easy method of reporting war vessels and data in one hoist.   It involved the use of the Pilot Jack *but not on the Jackstaff*.   It would be quite correct to fly a miniature house flag with a white surround.   As a youngster I made a couple of such flags for ships in which I was serving.

THE FOREMAST.   This carries a small signal yard some distance below the truck.   At the fore truck is flying the Spanish flag B, Fig. 24.2, the Spanish flag of 1910 not 1946, of course.   This is called the trading flag indicating the next country to be visited.   This flag will be changed a dozen times or more on the voyage at succeeding countries.   On the small signal yard is flying the Blue Peter, C, Fig. 24.2 (" I am about to sail ") the letter P in the International Code of Signals.   This will be *hauled down* smartly at the moment of casting off. If not at anchor or made fast *then the Blue Peter* should not be flown.   The complimentary flag is similar to the trading flag in that it is a foreign national flag flown at the foremast head of merchant ships.   When in a foreign port it is customary to fly *that* country's flag, but just before sailing the trading flag is flown along with the Blue Peter.   There is the strange case of the Allied Control Commission who were afloat on a British ship carrying out their duties in 1945-46 on the Dalmation coast.   Patriotism and pique were running high. There were four national representatives on board and each morning four national flags were hoisted to the fore truck simultaneously, foot by foot. They hung, all four flags together, quite undistinguishable, but none was superior or inferior to the other.

Still on the foremast on another halliard is the Royal Mail flag (D, Fig. 24.2) (" I have *His Majesty's* Mails on board ").   Occasionally one may see the Royal Mail flag (or its equivalent) of other countries.   It may surprise many to know that even in this century windjammers have carried His Majesty's Mails. This flag may also be flown on the jackstay above the bridge.

On occasion it may be found necessary to cross a special signal yard on the foremast, because there are two foreign ambassadors on board, taking up their appointments in their respective countries.   Each brings his own flag and as an act of courtesy their flags are hoisted, the senior diplomat's to starboard the junior's to port.   Neither takes exception to the Blue Peter being " superior " in a flag sense, hence the diplomacy of the company and ship's officers has avoided what might have been an awkward situation. Normally, in two-masted ships, ambassadors' flags are hoisted at the fore. It is unthinkable to have the trading flag (a national flag) superior, or even equal, to an ambassador's flag, and there might be some hurt national pride in the reverse position, so the trading flag is not displayed. An ambassador when taking passage between ports within his sphere of duty is clearly entitled to have his flag displayed.

THE MAINMAST. Being a large local liner there is no need to fly International Code " PT " (I want a pilot) or International Code " 5 " (same thing), or the pilot jack at the foremast head. As, however, the pilot *is already aboard* the white and red horizontally divided flag is hoisted above the bridge on the signal jackstay (F, Fig. 24.2), to indicate this fact. This red and white flag is kept flying while in pilotage waters with the pilot aboard. It is frequently and correctly flown in the lower rigging, main or mizzen. At the main mast head is the company's house flag (E, Fig. 24.2), an important and revered flag. The particular flag on this occasion has two tails (a burgee), because the master is the Commodore of the Company.

On the mizzen mast flies the ship's name pennant (G, Fig. 24.2). This is a very long pennant, usually in white, having the ship's name in prominent letters. This flag was a special feature on liners in the latter part of the nineteenth century, but has now gone out of fashion, not because of lack of pride by the seaman in his ship, but simply because of lack of masts.

There remains the fourth, or jigger mast. The flag at the truck follows no hard-and-fast rule. The master is an ardent member of some particular officers' association and he flies their flag (H, Fig. 24.2.) There was no difficulty in finding a flag to fly on the fourth mast. There is no gaff on the jigger mast so the Blue Ensign will fly at the ensign staff at the stern (J, Fig. 24.2.) The liner and master have the warrant to wear the Blue Ensign. This means that a certain number of officers and crew are members of the Royal Naval Reserve and that certain other conditions regarding the ship have been complied with.

Don't forget that warships, when at sea, fly the ensign at the peak, but in harbour they fly it at the ensign staff at or near the stern. Smart merchantmen do likewise if they have a gaff.

It will be seen that the foremast is overworked for flags. Right! We'll do away with the foremast altogether. We'll have only one mast, a mainmast. The modern liner usually has this mast forward of the single funnel (Fig. 24.3.) Instead of one yard we will now find two signal yards and on each of the four yardarms there are several halliards. Hoists may be made at the truck, the starboard upper yardarm, port upper yardarm, starboard yardarm, port yardarm, and finally on the fore and aft signal jackstay from the mainmast to the funnel. The positions are mentioned in their order of superiority.

73

When H.M.S. *Repulse* took their Majesties to Canada, in 1939, the one mast had to accommodate all the three flags usually worn when a warship carries the Sovereign. Viz, the Royal Standard at the truck, the flag of the Lord High Admiral to starboard, and the Union flag to port. In addition, of course, the White Ensign was worn aft and the Jack forward at the jackstaff (see Fig. 23.1).

CHAPTER FIFTEEN

Painting & finish-ing your model.

$\mathbf{T}$HE old " shellbacks " of the wind-jammers were fond of model making. Usually it was a model of the ship in which they were serving. Very often the lines of the hull were " sweet " and fairly accurate because the whole crew criticised, suggested, and helped. But when it came to the rigging it was done alone. Sailors do not presume to criticise each other's craftsmanship and seamanship. Nevertheless, the model was rigged correctly but seldom was the running gear correct *to scale*. A couple of reels of cotton had to serve for the whole model. The painting and the " finish " of the model was usually atrocious.

I have never had any difficulty in identifying a " sailor-made model." I made them myself in my younger days in the windjammers so I know of the sailorman's difficulties. Fortunately modellers ashore have better materials to hand and we have a few tricks. We can look over a coachpainter's shoulder and watch him get that wonderful " finish." If you can find one of the old coachpainters it would be well to cultivate his friendship. He has to use the " gun " (paint spray) it is true, and cellulose is something which was undreamt of in his seven year apprenticeship days.

Let us not waste time over the past glories of the coachpainter's craft. You want to have a superb finish to your model. There are certain elementary rules. The surface to be painted must have a true and smooth finish so far as tools can achieve this. Your paints should be of the finest quality procurable. A world famous firm of artists' colourmen were making, in the years before the war, a range of paints of excellent quality at sixpence or a shilling each pot. There were more than a score of different colours. I mention this to show that cost should not deter the modeller from striving for a fine finish.

Having prepared the surface for painting then apply good paints and rub down. The number of coats of paint depends to a great extent upon the *quality* of the paint and upon the kind of surface being painted.

Let us take a simple wooden hull, one piece of wood to be painted in one colour. It may be soft- or hardwood, heavily grained like pitch-pine or close-grained like boxwood. The heavy grain (foolish modeller to select such a wood) will require one, or maybe two, filler-coats. The filler-coat consists of powdered

75

slate or something of that kind. Its purpose is to fill up the spongy hollows between the hard lines of the grain. When your first filler-coat is dry then rub it down with very fine glass-paper. Maybe you have a fancy for some other rubbing-down material, but whatever you use be sure you rub down *to* the wood, but not *into* it. Later on, instead of fine sand-paper, you will use a damp chamois leather and powdered pumice stone. This pumice stone powder must be very fine, the sort used by dentists for teeth.

After your filler then apply your colour. Two thin coats are much better than one thick coat of paint. After *every* coat the surface must be rubbed down.

I do want to emphasise this point—a good quality paint, although apparently thin compared with some of the cheaper commercial paints, has a much greater covering power per coat. For a normal model you should have one filler coat and half a dozen colour coats, or less, according to the quality. There will be of course a rubbing between each coat. No coat should require more than 48 hours' drying time.

The modern trend of model finish is eggshell. It is now considered old fashioned to finish with a highly polished glossy surface, and with this I do agree. The glossy surface is a matter of some varnish—again, don't forget, it must be good quality varnish. It is not a bad idea to strain your varnish through a fine muslin. It takes time to do this.

One very important tip. All painting and varnishing, and, of course, the drying thereof, should be done in a room with windows and doors closed. You'd be surprised how much dust there is flying around. If your case for the model is ready then use it when drying coats of paint.

The foregoing remarks may be a revelation to those modellers who have been content to apply a couple of coats of paint, but they cannot have seen a good " finish " without wondering how and why. I am not exaggerating when I say that a really fine finish sometimes required a score of coats. However, the modern quality of paint manufactured by artists' colourmen has a greater covering power and is of finer texture. I doubt now if half a dozen coats are needed to achieve something like perfection. To do this requires careful and painstaking preparation of the surface. Make some special effort to secure the finest and best of rubbing down materials. A piece of dried sharkskin is perfection in this direction and in the old navy days the crews of the captain's gig and the admiral's barge in stations abroad always had some. *The painting and finish of your model should start as soon as reasonably possible. As models generally are built up, parts should be painted separately. It is most important when rubbing a flat surface with glass-paper to use a " bearer " or wrap the paper round another flat surface.* Alternatively rub the article on the paper itself. Rubbing down cannot be hurried. If you hurry you'll spoil the nice sharp edges of your workmanship.

Have you ever admired the perfect waterline which some modellers get ? It seems to be dead level with not a twist or a shake in it. There's no merging of the boot-topping paint with the top-side paint. Indeed, it looks almost as if the line between the two colours had been cut with a knife. Well, I suppose that could be true. They are two separate pieces of wood laminated. Having been painted separately, and being each a " true and smooth " surface, the perfect waterline is the result.

Here's another method. All good modellers take an early opportunity to fix their models to a base. Common sense dictates that the model shall be perfectly upright and on an even keel. By resting a pencil in a horizontal position on a block of wood it can be slid around on the base. By arranging to have the pencil point at the exact waterline height, presto, your waterline !

At this point there's some divergence of practice. Some people gum paper along the waterline. They can then paint quite freely the exposed part of the hull, some water, and off comes the paper. Others again use a razor blade resting on the line. Others are just like coach painters, they rely upon the perfect co-operation between the hand and the eye. Mark you well, it must be a steady hand and a true eye.

The painted ports of the nineteenth century windjammers present a problem to the novice. The general appearance is that of a wide white band along the side of the ship and on this band there are black oblong patches approximating in size to the gun ports of the earlier part of the nineteenth century. These painted ports are just a survival of the *ruse de guerre* used by the merchantmen against privateers and even warships. At a distance it would look as if the ship were pierced with gunports and many a merchantman was saved from capture thereby. However, the modeller has the awkward job of painting them in position.

I SUGGEST CIGARETTE PAPERS, but the application of cigarette papers should be by the gummed edge alone, otherwise the thin paper has a habit of literally falling to bits when wet all over. There are several types of adhesive tapes and papers which may be used. The use of a razor blade should not be overlooked. By far the best work I have seen in this direction came from the north-east coast. This patient modeller and facile craftsman *had inlaid his ports*. He had made an excellent job of it too. It will be seen from the foregoing that many people in the long run develop their own ideas. In my work of judging I frequently come across new ideas adopted by modellers to solve some minor problem.

Yes, that's it ! Solving some minor problem. Modelling a ship becomes, in due course, a series of minor problems surmounted in the most surprisingly varied manner. A friend of mine, who is an exceedingly clever engineer, had been wrestling with the idea of making sailing lights, or rather quarter lanterns for his seventeenth century ship. His wife had overheard from time to time his forceful but very undomestic language at the several failures to provide decorative tops to lanterns. One day she handed him the top of a scent spray affair bought in a sixpenny store. He presented her with two more sprays fitted with new tops made by himself to replace the originals. Looking at his model today in a well-known museum one would never dream—but modelling is like that. The work-basket, the junk-shop and the sixpenny store are the happy hunting grounds of the modeller.

" Brightwork," which is the sailor's name for varnished or oiled wooden rails, " houses," etc., is very often spoiled by poor varnish. My method is as follows. I thin out a very small quantity of gold size with methylated spirit. This is so thin that it goes on quickly, easily penetrates cracks and awkward corners. The spirit evaporates quickly leaving a thin but very even coat over all. It is so thin that the third application leaves a very clean but even coat which would satisfy the most critical. I have never tried this over a coat of paint, so be careful if you wish to experiment on a painted surface. *This is meant for use direct on to a raw wood surface requiring a varnish finish.* Highly suitable for dinghies and other small craft, first, because it does not clog up the plank overlaps and, second, because being a pure woodwork job, good workmanship can be displayed in the nude as it were. Little need be said about varnishing. Better too thin than too thick in consistency. Best quality only of course. The actual difference in cost for your model will be a fraction of a penny perhaps. A warm room temperature is helpful to the varnisher. Don't dilly-dally.

I was once asked the question " How many coats of paint must I apply in order to achieve a good finish ? " The governing factors are, (a) how well is your woodwork prepared for painting, and (b) what kind of wood is it. Your objective is to eliminate every possible " shadow " of the wood-grain coming or showing through. Some woods are soft, soggy, and " thirsty " between the grains. Miniature models may be " filled " with paint but for large models one or two coats of a filler will be a definite help. Then " coat and rub " until no grain shadow is visible. Check from plenty of viewpoints in strong light.

Mr. G. H. Draper (of Ilford), the well-known miniaturist, evolved a method of testing the consistency of paint. This method of his was originally created in connection with the range of colours specially prepared for ship modellers by Messrs. Reeves Ltd.,*the well-known artists' colourmen. Moreover, it was designed as a test for his own miniatures in the first place. I feel sure that Mr. Draper would only be too glad to know that his method had been of assistance to modellers, but at the same time it is as well to sound the warning that all paints are not of the same quality and therefore use only the principles of the test as a guide. The number of drops and the time factor is best decided by each individual. The object of the test is to determine how far your particular brand of paint may be " thinned down."

The ideal dipping rod might be made from a piece of steel or even from a butcher's wooden meat skewer, say 3 or 4 inches long, and ⅜ inch thick. The end should be tapered and pointed, as shown in Fig. 25.

By timing your drips from the stick when held vertically after a dip in your paint, you will have a standard as reference for future mixings.

The dipping rod must be kept very clean. Clean your brushes every time. Remove the surplus paint in paraffin or *genuine* turpentine. Wash in warm water and soap. See that your brushes do not have to stand " on their heads " all night.

Sable brushes are best. Hogshair are probably next. A sable brush will last a modeller all his life and will improve with age. Your artists' colourman will show you dozens of shapes and sizes. Content yourself with one round and one flat for a start. Experience will guide you later.

2½"   ½"

3/32" Dia   1/32" Dia

Fig. 25. Dipstick for testing consistency of paints

The Reeves special range of colours for Ship Modellers are no longer available.

CHAPTER SIXTEEN

Miniatures and prisoner~of~war models.

THE most pleasing model of all is the miniature. It is fascinating, and by its very nature of selection and rejection it is a work of art. Those who aspire to be miniaturists must master the secrets of selection, rejection and above all, suggestion. Possibly the last one is the most important of the three.

Here are a few tips to help you with some of the awkward jobs. The chapter " Dandyfunk " also has a hint or two useful to the miniature worker.

LIFEBOATS : Shape a stick of wood *across the grain* so that the section conforms to the plan of the boat. Carve the end of the stick into the bottom of the boat. Cut off and finish the top of the boat with two smooth surfaces representing the roof-like canvas cover. By this method, all boats are identical in length and plan shape.

WINCHES AND OTHER DECK DETAILS : Get a bird's-eye view of any deck fitting. Draw your object, say a windlass, in three views, plan elevation and end elevation. Shape the end of a piece of hardwood as end elevation, and with file, needle and knife, shape a " plan " and a front elevation. It may be advantageous to " stick on " awkward details such as, for example, drum-ends.

TOOLS : Old needles, broken or otherwise, may be converted into a series of useful tools such as awls, screw-drivers and chisels. Heat the end, shape it, heat again and at " cherry red " colour, plunge in water. This should give something which can be sharpened for small jobs. If in doubt, consult a handbook of tempering metals.

DOWELS AND PINS : Bamboo dowelling solves many troubles. Bamboo can be scraped down as fine as thread. Some prefer (in miniature work) to glue first then drill and dowel afterwards.

FUNNEL BAND: Run 3-amp fuse wire round the funnel, smear a little solder paste lightly along the wire. Hold in place by twisting at the back. Pass the funnel through gas ring flame once or twice, nip off twist and use, if necessary file very carefully. Hold your miniature together with pins, screws, and nuts and bolts. Don't depend on glue.

MINIATURE BULWARKS AND RAILS (SOLID) dead along the edge, say, round the bridge or a control tower, etc. Required: a little solder paste, bunsen burner or gas ring, old scissors, very fine gauge copper or brass foil.   Cut off foil to the required height and length.   Shape it to the plan very carefully. Lay this on a perfectly smooth piece of foil (the deck as it were), smear the 50/50 along the join.   Hold the whole quite level and pass it over the flame once or twice.   Cut off carefully and file.

MINIATURE RAILS (OPEN WORK).   Make a wooden frame of ample size. Score marks top and bottom to correct spacing of the vertical stanchions. Score marks at each end of the frame to correspond to the horizontal rails. Using very fine thread (to the correct scale of the horizontal rails) tie the end to one of the end frames, and coil the thread round the frame lengthways, one coil to each notch.   Now the vertical stanchions.   *First method* :—A single piece of thread for each one.   Tie the end to the top rail (clove hitch).   Pull it straight down with a touch of glue to hold the bottom end in position.   Put a spot of glue on the knot and also on each intersection of the " rails."   Use french polish, gold size, or paint to stiffen the whole " rail."   The vertical stanchions must have " roots " an eighth to a quarter extra length.   Cut and trim the whole from the frame.   The threads at the back of the frame are

H.M.S. Prince, 1670

" waste" *To fix on hull,* insert the roots into cuts in the side of the hull. If for a line of rails across the deck then insert the roots into pinholes. (Kellar, Glasgow.)

Second method :—For vertical stanchions. Clove hitch in the middle so that two ends hang down. Twist the ends to form a thicker vertical railpost, being careful to have the same number of twists between each horizontal rail. Use bottom end " roots " as before.

Third method :—Use suitable gauge wire and a little solder paste. In all cases be careful not to disturb the tension of the horizontal rails. Very few people ever made a perfect job the first time. If in any doubt about the quality—do it again.

Fourth method :—Cut very thin celluloid to the required shape and length, and on the celluloid paint, or draw the " rails." Celluloid may also be used for the making of catapults in naval vessels, cranes and towers in the same manner as for the rails, viz., draw the girder and lattice work on the celluloid. To join celluloid use amyl acetate as a solvent. Your local cinema projectionist will explain the joining of celluloid pieces.

It is good to plan your miniature on " make or break " lines. The hull should be in parts, e.g., keel to waterline, waterline to main, or any convenient deck. Fo'c'sle-head centre island and poop ; the main parts are held by nuts and bolts. Yes, I'm not forgetting we are talking about miniatures, but that is the Draper method. Hampshire, on the other hand, *does* build up " for keeps." Hampshire makes much use of mapping pens, pens and artists' brushes.

I have found, however, that miniaturists more than any others, develop their own individuality. In your first month you'll know if you will be a good miniaturist.

FRENCH PRISONER-OF-WAR MODELS

While discussing miniatures, it is well worth mentioning the French prisoner-of-war models.

During the Napoleonic Wars, there were three main camps for the French prisoners of war. They were at Dartmoor, Porchester and Norman's Cross. Liverpool, however, " housed " a considerable number, mostly captured sailors, and their prison was in Great Howard Street. Owing mainly to economic conditions, the prisoners were permitted to earn money by selling the results of their handiwork. An important item was the sale of ship models. Models were made at all the camps in various small scales, say, models of 6 in. to 24 in. long. It is true to say that some of the prisoners spent nearly half their lives in captivity, and much of their handiwork is still to be seen in various museums. They were restricted in their choice of materials, but they made excellent use of what was available, namely—bone from their meat meals, straw from their palliasses, human hair, scraps of wood, and possibly some things from the butcher's shop in the prison. Some years ago, I was entrusted

R.M.S. Caronia   Picture by Donald McNarry

with the work of examining and annotating the prisoner-of-war models in the City of Liverpool Museums and Shipping Gallery. Extracts from my notes, therefore, may be of interest. For reasons of space I will confine myself to the *Pilkington Collection of Miniature Ship Models.** These are, I think, the finest example of miniatures in the country and they appear to be almost exclusive to Liverpool. There are some examples to be found elsewhere, but the twenty-two models in the collection gave me ample scope for analysis. There were at least four different modellers concerned, and they quite unmistakably showed their personality in their models. As to the models themselves, the majority are made from wood, wood chips and shavings. Most are fitted with sails made of wood shaving so thin that lights and windows show through. The scale of these models is generally about one in eight hundred or less. One of them, see accompanying photograph, is to the approximate scale of one in thirteen hundred, with an overall length of less than 3 in. This is a French " 74 " with a hull just 2 in. in length. The sails appear to be yellow pine mellowed by age (a century and a half now) to the colour of mahogany. *The ropes are also made from wood.* All the masts and spars are perfectly proportioned. The decks are built. Each of the guns is mounted on its own carriage which in turn is fitted with wheels. Ladders are complete with handrails and steps. Here are some general items about these models. The gunports were 1/25 in. square and the port-lids were triced up in a proper seamanlike manner. The boat in the stern davits contained thwarts and oars. The quarter galleries had their latticed windows and balustraded rails. There was in each case a figurehead. Note, too, the carving of the statues on the plinth, the floor of which had a complicated pattern of coloured straws.

The models were each mounted on an ornamental base of an intricate and highly decorative nature. Some of these bases have an angel at each corner and each angel is complete with wings and a trumpet.

How would you like to carve a naval ensign out of shavings alone ? These bygone captive Frenchmen did it, *and to the scale of their model, too.*

So much for the wooden models, and it will not be forgotten that some of these models were only as long as half a cigarette. Others in the collection were of bone saved from their meals. Not all the rigging was of chip wood. Mostly it was made of silk. There were some examples of very fine human hair, silvery and silky.

But the most remarkable model of the lot was that one known popularly as the " *mother-of-pearl* " model.

Its scale was similar to the majority, about one in eight hundred, i.e., 1 in. to 66 ft. The real attraction was its glistening white appearance, as if made of mother-of-pearl. To modellers, however, there remains the mystery. What was the material or treatment ? The hull and solid parts may have been lime-

* See illustration of one of the models in the Pilkington Collection.

Prisoner-of-War model (*French*), 1802—4   *Picture by the Port of Liverpool Shipping Gallery, City of Liverpool Museum.*

bleached bone, but I could not determine this for certain. They were polished obviously. When we examine the sails, however, the mystery deepens, because they were almost transparent. The possibility of mica flakes or sea-shell flakes may be dismissed at once. So too, perhaps more reluctantly, we can dispose of the possibility that hardened intestinal remains of certain animals were used.

There is a strong probability that the horns of a cow supplied the material. The horns, when boiled, become very soft and can be peeled off in very.thin flakes. Carefully selected layers might then be beaten between leathers, as in the manner of the gold beater, followed by a bleaching and a polishing. It may be inferred that the work was exceedingly difficult because no other example of this kind of work is in the collection. Moreover, the model bears evidence that it was experimental because some of the head and for'ard sails show signs of discolouration and are duller and heavier in texture. These differences in appearance are slight today and probably at the time would not be noticeable at all. It would seem to confirm that the craftsman was endeavouring to attain some degree of permanence in whiteness and polish. In this he, or perhaps they, succeeded beyond all question. The perfection of detail in this model is quite equal to the best in the collection. The deadeyes, for example, are correctly pierced with their three holes and the deadeye is 1/100 in. in diameter.

Another interesting item is that this is one of the few models to be fitted with studding sails. These sails, of course, as most readers know, were only used in very fine weather and were extensions on the outside edges of the normal sails. An ingenious method was used to hold them in position. Long supporting stays stretch from the studding sails right across the ship right down to the outer edge of the baseboard. As very fine silvery hair was used for this, it is only after a very keen search that they can be seen.

If you should pass through Liverpool, do not miss this collection in the Port of Liverpool Shipping Gallery, of the City of Liverpool Museum, in William Brown Street.

CHAPTER SEVENTEEN

Setting your
model in a sea.

$\mathbf{M}$ANY people like the waterline
model. Such a model must be set in a sea and these notes on " seas " will
help you.

What is known as a " wave " to landsmen is called a " sea " by sailors.

The simplest sea of all is plain blue or green glass, or even plain blue-green
or grey silk. These, however, have their limitations. They are only to be
used for ships at anchor or in very placid circumstances. Any of them could
be used for a ship which is becalmed. This, however, is extremely risky.
In many, many years' experience, I have only twice known the ocean to be
absolutely mirror-smooth, free from rollers and without the blemishing shadow
from even a capful of wind.

To show a calm sea in mid-ocean there's plenty of coloured glass with just
a very slight undulation. This is also suitable for ships at anchor in a road-
stead.

There's a more complicated form to be described ; that is the size and shape
of the " sea " (wave). Many people get their idea of a " sea " from the seaside
beach. These are " breakers " caused by the land friction checking the bottom
of the " sea," and the momentum of the top of the " sea " carrying on and
falling over in a crest. What you see at Brighton is the very small brother of
the surf at Durban, Honolulu or some other surf-bound beach. The ocean
roller travels maybe a thousand miles. Approaching the shallow water, it
turns into a breaker and causes the surf. The roller is just simply a big wave
which has travelled on by its momentum long after the wind-storm has gone,
maybe in another direction, or has merely died away. The roller loses much
of the height it had when it was a wave. One can compare the roller to the
wave as the Downs of Southern England to the Grampians of Scotland. It
is as well to study seas on any lucky opportunity. Even from the end of a pier
or breakwater is better than nothing. Also keep a " cuttings " book of " seas "
comprised of either photographs or reproductions of paintings by recognised
marine artists.

ONCE AGAIN I MUST WARN YOU. Take no notice of the long white wave on
the sand at the seaside.

87

Generally speaking, seas follow roughly the same proportions, whether 6 feet or 36 feet high. (See Fig. 26.)

Now what is a sea ? It is sufficient for us modellers to say that the force of wind disturbs the surface of the ocean. The more the force and the longer it flows the greater the disturbance. The wind is never steady in direction and force. This causes differences in the size of the seas in any given area.

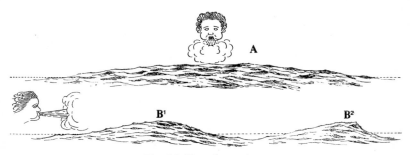

Fig. 26. Wave formation

Moreover, currents, tides, shallow water and the proximity of rocks all have their effects upon seas. The normal heavy sea of a gale in the " roaring forties " or the North Atlantic is 30 feet high from trough to crest in a vertical measurement. It is quite true to say that three big seas come together.

In a half-hour's observation one might count a hundred seas at 20 feet, three or four groups at 30 feet, with a couple or so at 40 feet. I have seen seas of 50 feet in the several stormy stretches of the oceans. Reliable observers have noted seas 60 feet high.

Let us examine one sea. It will be 800 feet along the axis. The windy side of the sea will be a very long easy slope, say 400 feet from the peak back to the lowest part of the trough behind. Now the front of the wave has a much steeper slope, as will be seen in Fig. 26B. As more and more water gets pushed up the hill there comes a time when it is pushed right over the top and so we get the crest or break of the sea. Fig. 26B2. Actually, it is not the water that moves *but the shape of the water.* Consequently, when the crest breaks the foam so caused is left behind. Our 800 feet sea is travelling at a speed of 12-15 knots. These crests are usually small affairs of a few tons of water on a frontage of 10 to 30 feet. Sometimes the wind is so strong that the crest is blown away in fine spray so that the appearance generally resembles a low lying mist.

It follows then if you want to show a good sea you must take plenty of room. In Fig. 27, for example, although I show eight seas they are crowded together too much. The distances apart should be twice as much as shown. The ship is shown hove-to on the port tack. In this sketch are shown also the crest just curling A, samples of a break B, and the positions of foam after a break C. D indicates the foam merging into the waves now forming. Obviously, there is no level surface, every square foot being a part of one or other of the seas. For the artist, the brighter the sunlight, the deeper or more intense should be the colour. This is usually green or blue ; with an overcast sky, the prevailing colour would be gray. Quite often a howling gale is accompanied by bright sunshine.

So much for the seas. The position of the ship in a sea requires examination. It is possible to portray speed and action by the judicious use of waves and foam caused by the ship herself. But again one must take account of the

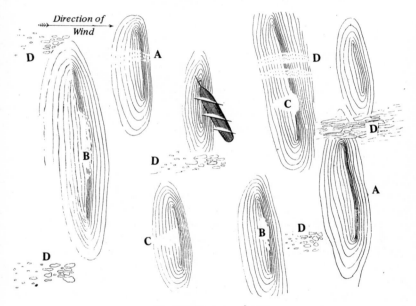

Fig. 27. A group of seas

direction of the wind and, what is even more important, the direction of the sea.

I can say this about the sea. Any modeller who cares to sit down quietly and plan out his sea setting will, without any doubt, evolve a setting worth while. A ship causes the following characteristic water disturbances (refer to Fig. 28). *The bow wave* (M) (or bone in her teeth) is to be found at almost any speed and in any size of ship. In smooth water it would be a regular arrowhead slightly

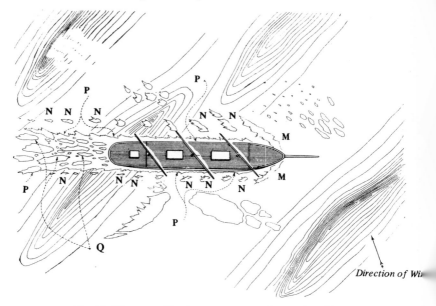

Fig. 28. Diagram of broken water around a moving ship

curved outwards. There is a *false bow wave* (N) caused by the chopping action of the bows as they pitch down into an oncoming sea. *The true wake* (P) commences well for'ard and is ten to twenty inches wide in normal ships, depending upon the speed. The greater the speed the wider the wake. This wake is made up of the bubbles and the disturbance of water in friction with the skin of the ship. The wake arriving at the stern is joined with the greater disturbance of the water rushing in under the counter. This part (Q) is indicated by *smooth* boiling patches of water, dark green or dark blue or even grey. A couple of circular smooth patches slightly convex, but only slightly, size, say quarter beam. Watch when your cross channel steamer turns sharply. You'll see the polished patch I mean. Now here's another headache, *the reflected* sea. The false bow wave is one type. The stern crushing down causes others, and then there's the case of a medium sea striking the ship and, not being big enough to pour aboard or lift the ship, is thrown off again at the appropriate angle, as, for example, in the manner of a billiard ball on the cushion. Study carefully the sketches. " Period ship " workers as a rule do not make waterline models, but if you do, be careful not to have too much sail ; the crusaders did not " crack on."

Here are five sketches of the varying amounts of sail carried by an early windjammer. (See Fig. 29.) Heavy weather (o) is an addition of my own to the orthodox quartette of full sail (M), plain sail (N), storm sail (P), and bare poles (Q). Very little explanation is necessary here. A ship might run before a whole gale under bare poles ; most ship masters, however, would heave-to under storm sail. Under-manned ships would be compelled to heave-to under almost any heavy weather conditions. Emigrant ships to the colonies, and wool clippers which usually had double crews and stout gear, would often run before a moderate or even a strong gale under plain sail. To me that was the

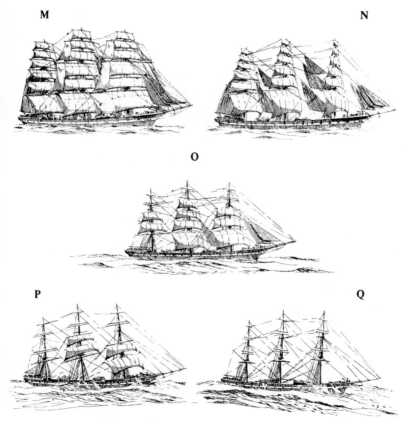

Fig. 29. Sketches showing sail carried under various conditions

USEFUL GUIDE TO SAIL, SEAS AND SPEED

WIND			SHIPS AND THEIR SAILS						SEAS	
Force No. (Beaufort Scale)	Description	Speed m.p.h.	Coastal Craft	Medieval	Tudor & Stuart Ships	Napoleonic Ships	Packets Clippers P. Liners	Windjammers	State	Height
0	Calm	0	—	Sweeps or oars	—	Towed by boats	Courses up in bunt-lines	Courses up in bunt-lines	Mirror Smooth	0
1	Light airs	1-3	Steerage way only	Sweeps or oars	—	Steerage way only	All sail set	All sail set steerage way only	Small waves, no foam	0-6 in.
2	Light breeze	4-6	1-2 knots	Steerage way	Steerage way	All sail set	All sail set	All sail set 2 knots	Small crests, no white	2 ft.
3	Gentle breeze	7-10	Slight heel	All sails set	All sail set, heeling	All sail set	All sail set, heeling	All sail set, 3-4 knots	Small crests, no white	2-5 ft.
4	Moderate breeze	11-16	Full sail and heeling	All sail set	All sail set, heeling	Take in kites	Take in stuns'ls	Heeling, take in royals, 5 knots	Small White horses	5-9 ft
5	Fresh breeze	17-21	Shorten sail	Shorten down	Shorten down	Take in royals except in chase	Take in stuns'ls	Take in to'gan'sls 8 knots	White foam crests	9-15 ft.
6	Strong breeze	22-27	Reef sails	Shorten down	Seek shelter	Take in to'gan'sls except in chase	Take in royals	Take in cro'jack 11 knots	Heavier foam crests	18 ft.

No.	Name	Knots							Sea	Height
7	Moderate gale	28–33	Off home	Under bare poles	Seek shelter	1st reefs in tops'ls	Take in to'gan'sls	Double tops'ls and fore course only 9 knots	Long streaks from foam crests	22 ft.
8	Fresh gale	34–40	Seek shelter anywhere	—	Under bare poles	2nd reefs in tops'ls	Take in to'gan'sls	Lower top'-sls only 7 knots	Great foam patches, crests blown away	26 ft.
9	Strong gale	41–47	—	—	—	Take in courses	Take in cro'jack & main course	Hove to	Spray flying from wave tops	31 ft.
10	Whole gale	48–55	—	—	—	Hove to	Double top'-sls & fore course only	—	Air filled with spray	37 ft.
11	Storm	56–65	—	—	—	Bare poles	3 lower top'-sls & fore course only	—	Air filled with spray	45 ft.
12	Hurricane	Over 65	—	—	—	—	3 lower top'sls only	—	Dense flying spray from foam	Over 45 ft.

quintessence of thrill, unknown to those who depend upon engines for propulsion, whether by land, sea or air.

Now some remarks on the materials. First, the very first choice should be carved soft wood. Add paint as required. Here are other successfully used materials. Papier-mache (i.e., pulped paper) putty, plasticene, toffee and clay. I've seen them all, but wood carving is best.

On an idea suggested by Mr. D. S. Anthes, of Sheffield, I have compiled a table based on a mixture of official sources (Beaufort scale, Admiralty Manual of Seamanship) and my own experience which, perhaps, may be of some use to modellers in adjusting the relationship between speeds, winds, sail carried, and condition of the sea. It can only be regarded as a guide because no two masters are alike in their judgment, caution, skill, courage, and foolishness.

To use this table intelligently, I would suggest that the modeller should build up his data by enquiry and research. For example, a ship close hauled and a ship running before the wind, each would require different treatment, but the table does indicate how his queries should be framed when seeking detailed information. If he asks sailors, the answers generally speaking will differ, but by listening patiently he can then safely use his own judgment.

The packets were driven, the clippers were well manned (mostly double crews). The German P liners of the period following the first world war, were driven *and* well manned. The P liners, by the way, made remarkably fast and consistent voyages, Europe to W.C.S. America, which for some strange reason have never been widely recognised.

The windjammers (excluding the P liners) were undermanned, cheaply run, deficient in stores and equipment, and this is reflected in my table, in spite of the fact that I personally took part in a record passage, which I believe still remains unbroken. (Ship : *Brenda*, 1,995 tons. Diamond Head, Honolulu, to Nobbies, N.S.W., Australia, 26 days, October-November, 1905. Master : James Learmont.)

As an instance, the *Lawhill* was originally built for a crew of 42, yet for years she had well under 30 hands all told, and I believe at one time was down to 24 hands. Small wonder royals were furled in a moderate breeze outside the " Trades."

CHAPTER EIGHTEEN
Cases for your models.

AT a fairly early stage in model making one becomes aware of the necessity for some protection for the model. It may be because of children, or even kittens. Not so many years ago I found the feline pet on a shelf contentedly chewing the tarred rigging of a contemporary model (1840).

Sometimes, too, a model is to be displayed (in its incomplete state) to a friend or to the local society. Here is where the transport case comes in.

THE TRANSPORT CASE (see Fig. 30A), is inexpensive. It is easy to make, and in it a model may be packed or unpacked in a matter of seconds—and quite safely too, for a journey from Land's End to John o' Groats, if necessary. My description will be brief, but in conjunction with the sketches, it should be sufficient to explain the idea.

The case has four plywood sides with wooden base and wooden top. One of the plywood sides is hinged at the bottom, and thus lies flat when open. On the base or underside of the case are fixed two ⌐ shaped runners to hold a light baseboard. One pair of chocks may be fitted on this light sliding baseboard if desired. The model is held by light lashings (or indiarubber bands) to small hooks in the baseboard on either side of the model. The case has a broad base and a small top. There is a pronounced taper, especially for rigged sailing ships. A light rope or strap fitted round the case (including the opening side) ends in two loops on top for easy carrying. This rope is secured to the case on the outside by a few small wire lashings, each through two tiny holes on either side of the rope. Two lashings on either side of the case are sufficient. The splice may be one of the handles. The baseboard obviously will also be your working baseboard. There must be no " play " in the baseboard. An eyebolt screw will solve this. Details are left to each individual.

Now let us examine some other types of cases all of which are for exhibition purposes. Broadly there are two classes ; the *passe-partout* for small models, such as miniatures and " one-foot " *scenics*, and the framed exhibition case of fine wood.

Some of the " one-foot scenics " require a case 15 in. × 6 in. × 15 in., and this is really the top limit of size carried out in *passe-partout*. At this size, too, the case must be well made. *Passe-partout* simply means joining and holding pieces of glass with sticky or adhesive tape. Special tapes are sold for this specific purpose. They are obtained in various colours so that a modeller can improve the appearance of his work by an artistic choice of coloured tape. If in doubt, play for safety and use black or dark grey. There are certain points to be emphasised in making your *passe-partout* case. It is in two main portions, the glass and the base plus model. The glass fits into a groove about a quarter of an inch deep. The fit must be good and dustproof. Therefore, line your groove with black velvet if your fitting is not to your liking. Glass is obtainable as sheet glass (pictures and domestic windows) or plate glass (shop fronts and countertops). It is sold by area and in sheet glass there are several weights of which these three are in common commercial use, viz., 18 oz., 24 oz., and 32 oz. An 18-oz. glass might be used for small models. The weight in ounces refers to the weight of a square foot.

Plate glass is much heavier and more expensive. It also is sold by area. A square foot of plate glass weighs from 3 lb. to 4 lb., at $\frac{1}{4}$ in. thick, and, of course, twice that weight at $\frac{1}{2}$ in. thick. During a talk with the general manager of Messrs. J. Preedy & Sons Ltd., of Ashland Place, London W.1 , I gathered quite a few tips on glass. This firm handles anything from cathedral stained glass windows to cucumber frames. His first advice to all amateur case makers was, go to your local library and spend an hour with a technical book, on, for instance, stained glass, for valuable tips. He also reminded me that such home books as the *Handyman and Home Mechanic* would be very helpful.

Let us make a *passe-partout* model-case. The first essential is accurate measurement and a very accurate cutting, with the corners dead square. It will save a tremendous amount of time to make a box or skeleton frame to the correct *inside* measurements of the glass. This case may be used to hold the glass in position while applying the tape. How wide is your tape ? That is a matter of taste, but it helps a lot to put a crease down the middle. Don't forget to allow for that part of *the glass in the groove* when making your template box. Finally : see that the glass top (always glass on top, please) fits *over* the sides and not *inside* the sides.

Cutting glass is a question of practice, so take my tip and get some practice. The wheel is equally as good as the diamond in the hands of the amateur. Be bold and firm. If you show any fear the glass will find it out. *Accurate measurement*, and cut accurately *first time*. Hold the wheel upright and use more pressure than with a diamond. Be sure the glass lies on a perfectly flat surface. A blanket under the glass is an advantage, especially in the heavier weights. *One cut only*, not two or three. One firm, even, well-pressed stroke with the wheel upright all the time. Lay the glass with the cut along the straight edge which you have used. Spread a hand over the glass lying on the straight edge, then press suddenly on the other part. A gentle tapping beforehand on the outside of the cut will help in obstinate cases. If there is only a narrow strip to come away, use a finger and thumb firmly on either side of the cut with a bending and pulling away movement of the fingers. Use carborundum stone for smoothing off the nasty rough edges. When ready to apply the tape, first place the sides of the case around the " template " box or skeleton frame and tie string or tape vertically round the whole so as not to get in the way of the taping operation. Finally, " tape on " the top piece to the sides. It is a sensible idea to defer cutting the top piece of glass until the sides are joined up.

Don't forget that the glass cutting wheel can be sharpened up if it is dull. At the correct angle run it along the slate or stone a few dozen times. Sharpen it on both sides, of course.

The Metal Frame Exhibition Case.

The advancing popularity of the metal frame has much to recommend it. It is light, comparatively inexpensive, and suitable for cases with sides up to 3 ft. Such firms as Bond's or Buck & Ryan's, in Euston Road, can supply the angle metal in all sizes. Here is a guide to sizes. The longest side to your case is the factor. 12 in. side requires $\frac{3}{16}$ in. size of angle leg with 1/32 in. thickness of metal. $\frac{1}{4}$ in. and $\frac{1}{16}$ in. respectively is safer. A 2 ft. side should have $\frac{1}{2}$ in. and 3/32 in. The difficult job is soldering the corners together. Clean accurate cutting is necessary, and it must be remembered that three ends are joined together at each operation. Major Castle-Smith's method,

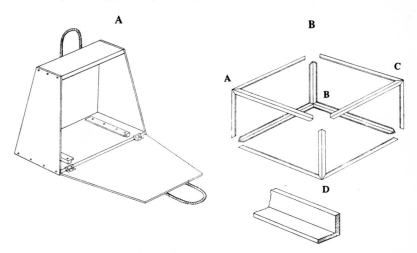

Fig. 30. Transport case

Ship Modelling Hints and Tips

as described in *Ships and Ship Models*, for November, 1938, was as follows : The two sides are clamped on a block of asbestos and the upright part is held in a special clamp. It is well worth making a special clamp for the purpose. The general idea is a wooden " foot " having a vertical bar on which is an arm to slide up and down and be clamped at the correct height. The end of the arm has an angled plate with a conveniently placed cross-bar fitted with a screw. This screw presses the piece to be soldered against the angled place. Make the joints at A, B, C, D first, see Fig. 30B, thus producing four units. " True " and square carefully every side after soldering the four units together.

Having removed all surplus solder, you are now ready for cementing the glass in position, for which a suitable glass cement should be used. It helps to key the cement if the metal angles are roughened with coarse emery cloth.

A golden rule. Insert one piece of glass at a time and allow the cement to set well for about half a day. Here are some suggested glass cements (i.e., glass to brass).

(1) Ordinary chalk and shellac varnish to a thick consistency.

(2) Three parts dry litharge (PbO) to one part (in weight) of glycerine. Sets in an hour.

The large wooden-framed exhibition case can be a job as big as the model itself. There are scores of different types of cases. I would suggest you go to the nearest museum or shipping company's office and examine some of the cases.

Whenever you send your model in a glass case by any form of transit it is advisable to paste on, in a criss-cross fashion, some two-inch roller bandage or stiff brown paper. It will not stop the glass being broken but it may prevent the broken glass from damaging your model.

* *Buck and Ryan's are now to be found at 101 Tottenham Court Road, London, W.1.*

CHAPTER NINETEEN
Dandyfunk~
Odds and ends.

DANDYFUNK was the name given by sailors in the windjammers to that wonderful dish of Friday afternoons. Into it went everything which was left over ; pickles, pork, molasses, biscuits, etc. It is not suggested that this chapter covers all that is left over, but here are some items to make an interesting and varied dish.

BLOCKS

Blocks cause much confusion in the mind of the novice modeller. A block may be just a knot or a blob of dark glue, or it may be an elaborate affair of cheeks, score, sheave, arse, strop and, indeed, the whole thing. Your blocks will, of course, conform to the scale. Modellers frequently use " suggestion " but how can you suggest a thing if you are not quite clear about the details of what you are suggesting ?

Figs. 31 and 32 include drawings of various blocks which, perhaps, may be useful to those working in the larger scales.

There are many different kinds of blocks each having its proper purpose. Some are bound with iron, others with wire, and some are held in an eye-splice. The important thing to remember is that the rope enters the lips of the block near the head and not towards the arse. It is a very common mistake to pierce holes in the centre.

On the page of old-time blocks (Fig. 31), A shows a Roman block and dead-eye of the first century. B is an early English deadeye, such as was used up to Elizabethan times, and C a seventeenth century deadeye. D is a sixteenth century block for a simple whip, E is the seventeenth century version of this, and F an eighteenth century buntline bridle. G is an early eighteenth century clewline block, and H is a sheet block of the same period. " Sheaves of brass " were used in ships in the sixteenth century.

Fig. 32P shows the various parts of an ordinary nineteenth century wooden block. The grooves on the outside are intended to take a " seized " strop or to hold the eye of an eyesplice. In the right hand view the cheeks have been opened out to show the sheave, the whole is held together with four large nails, one on each corner, the ends in each case being riveted over a washer.

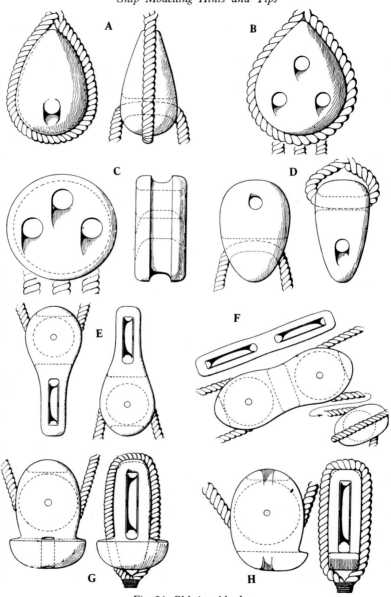

Fig. 31. Old-time blocks

Sheaves were sometimes made of lignum-vitae. Modern sheaves are mounted on ball bearings. One end of the pivot point is squared and the point is held in by nailing two small pieces of tin over the ends. Usually strops and eyesplices on blocks are wormed, parcelled, served and tarred ; to the modeller, this means a good coating of black shiny paint.

The head sheet block (Q, Fig. 32) is sometimes known as a clump block ; it is made from one piece of wood and is completely ovoid in shape, having no corners to catch into obstructions. When the ship changes tack, the sheets have to be payed over a stay. It is an urgent job and there must be no holdup. The size of the block varies from 9-12 inches.

The heavy three- or four-fold purchase block is an important piece of windjammer equipment ; it will be found as part of the fore and main tack tackle, the fish tackle and cat falls. It is iron-bound, and the moving block has a large hook formed on the strop. The illustration Fig. 32R, shows the standing block ; the usual size was from 15-18 in. long. The drawing shows a four-fold block, but the three-fold was the one carried on most windjammers.

The bumkin (Fig. 32T) is a feature on many windjammers. It is fixed outside the hull, well aft on the quarter just above main deck level. It gave a reasonable lead to the lower main brace, which otherwise would have been almost up and down on the lee side. Moreover, it enabled the watch to work on the main deck. In port the blocks were unhooked and the bumkin swung aft to be clear of dock walls, etc.

The pedestal mounted brace-lead blocks (Fig. 32U) were usually found on windjammers. These avoided the use of longish pendants outside the ship, they swivelled on a longitudinal axis. The pedestals were attached to the pin rail. The usual sizes of brace-lead blocks were with the course 15 in., lower tops'l 12 in., and upper tops'l 9 in.

The cargo gin block (Fig. 32S) is an all-iron block for wire cargo runners and is absolutely essential to merchant ships of all kinds, while working the cargo in port. At sea, all such things are stored away. The diameter of the sheave is from 12-16 in.

Make your blocks out of boxwood or holly. Carve and work the block at the end of a stick and when finished just cut it off and start on the next block. Model blocks are made from one piece as a rule. The good modeller will make a groove on each side of the block and then drill through near the top. For the stropping of metal bound blocks use soft copper wire. It can be flattened easily. If in doubt about the size of the block, use a block whose length is approximately four times the circumference of the rope which passes through it.

To make lower deadeyes and chain plates (see Fig. 33, sketch 4), take a round stick very slightly larger than the deadeye (A), soft wire (C) flattened with a hammer tap, a little solder paste, and several turns of thin wire stropping (B). Insert the stick into suitable base. Turn the end of the flattened soft wire over into a very small hook. Lay the flattened wire with the hook end touching the round stick. Take two or three turns of the thin wire stropping round the stick so that the thin wire also engages the hook of the flattened wire. Smear Solder apply bunsen burner. Remove carefully from the stick. Close the hook of the flattened wire. You should now have a piece of flattened wire with the top end curled back and holding firmly in its " curl " a circular coil of thin wire. The ends of the thin wire have, of course, been snipped off. Insert the " scored " deadeye (A) into the circle (B) and squeeze the loop (D) to the same width as the flattened soft wire (C). This was the method devised by the late Armitage McCann, of New York.

Decks of American elm and lined with pencil. Deckhouses of satin walnut if to be left " bright." For a first-class model of a ship involving fairly extensive decks, it is quite impossible to get camber and sheer out of one piece of wood, however thin it might be. The only alternative is decking by planks. Normal practice aboard ship is 4-inch planks, but one could use strips of wood say ten " planks " wide by using a scriber and rubbing in a suitable stuff to represent caulking. Butts should be over the thwartship beams. Be sparing in representing butts.

Eyebolts in the deck may be made thus : Choose a suitably sized pin from your box of " butterfly " pins. Bend the point over with tweezers. Cut off shank 1/8" or so. Stick shank into pierced hole. Set up your stay, backstay, or whatever it is and then 'drive home' your eyebolt firmly, thus at the same time setting up your stay 'bar-taut'.

Figureheads, see Bibliography.

Capstans. Fig. 34A shows the capstan of a first-rate ship of the eighteenth and early nineteenth centuries. The shaft of the capstan was carried through the upper deck and was provided with two heads, as shown, so that a double crew could be employed on it. Fig. 34C is the main capstan, as found on the fo'c'sle head of a windjammer, and 34B is the brace and halliard capstan, four of which were usually provided on the main deck. The main capstan was often fitted with a double tier of holes for capstan bars.

Steering wheel, Fig. 35A, shows a typical steering wheel for a windjammer. The diameter over the tips of the spokes was 6 ft., and the wheel had 12 spokes, which were fitted to square holes in the hub. One spoke has a tiny brass cap on the end, and when this is uppermost, it indicates the mid-ship position of the helm *exactly,* but don't forget that from one side to the other the wheel makes about seven revolutions. The brass cap is really a guide to the steersman in the dark. A common remark was " The ship is carrying three and a half spokes of weather helm," or " Five spokes of lea helm." This means that the average position of the brass cap would be three-and-a-half or five spokes from

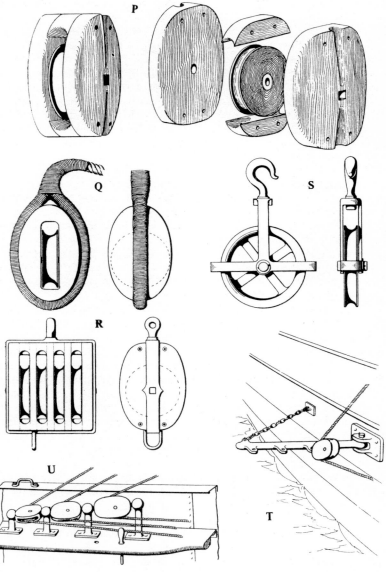

Fig. 32. Modern blocks

the top-centre. The rim of the wheel is reinforced by brass rings which are inlaid on each side of the wooden rim ; the front of the iron hub is covered with a brass cap. The 5-ft. wheel has 10 spokes and the 4-ft. wheel has 8 spokes.

The binnacle, which is shown on Fig. 35B, consists of a wooden or iron column, the top of which is surmounted by the brass cap which covers the compass ; the compass is illuminated by lamps on either side which are dropped into brass sockets formed on the compass cover. An oval sloping glass window is provided on the after side of the brass dome, through which the compass may be seen. Brackets on either side are provided to carry the soft iron balls which help to insulate the compass from the effects of ironwork on the ship. The binnacle was approximately 4 ft. high. The illustration shows the type in general use toward the end of the nineteenth century.

FUNNEL AND FUNNEL MARKINGS

A solid funnel with a bolt for a " root " and a nut to hold it firmly, is desirable in the smaller scales.

Wide bands of colour. Two narrow bands made as already described in Chapter XVI and paint between.

Change of funnel markings. In a period of twenty years a company may change its funnel markings and its house flag several times. Check your funnels with the date or year. No attempt is made in this book to describe various funnels. *See* Bibliography.

Mast hoops for fore and aft rig. Use shavings to make these hoops. Trim a stick to a slightly greater diameter than the mast. Wrap around it two sheets of thin waxed paper. Lay your shavings layer by layer over the waxed paper until the shaving has enough turns for your hoop thickness. Allow to dry thoroughly. Cut off with razor blade to correct size and extract the waxed paper.

A simple jig for ladders. Fig. 36 shows a hardwood jig for ladder making. Cuts are made to the size and angle of the tread or step. Each scale, of course, requires its own jig. Small ladders may be made from Bristol board. For large ladders cut a stick *across the grain* so that the section is the size and shape of your tread. Now chop off treads to the required thickness. Place the treads in the slots of the jig. A spot of your own favourite glue on the ends of the treads, then press your side piece into position.

If you use Bristol board, *colour it first.* Much trouble will be saved by attaching handrails on to your side pieces *before* attaching to treads. The normal size of a tread space is 14 in. centre to centre.

Portholes. Drill your holes cleanly to correct size. In practice the inside of a scuttle (Navy talk) or porthole (Merchant Service talk) is white, with perhaps a dark shadow striking downwards. Paint the inside white, and if you've a fancy then strike a dark or black shadow there as well. Some portholes are open and some are shut.

Fill up the hole with a clear adhesive and the appearance is strikingly like a closed porthole.

Good class stationers usually stock " Metal " paper eyelets, $\frac{1}{8}$ in. diameter, and they may also have other sizes. These may solve your porthole problem. Each one has a flange. Shoemakers' suppliers stock shoe eyelets in larger sizes.

Ratlines. A quick method of " rattling down." Centre the ratline in position on the first shroud or backstay. Do a round turn. Twist the two parts of your ratline up to the next shroud, then again a round turn with one of the parts. Twist the two parts again. Finish off on the last shroud with clove hitch. It is advisable to wet the finger tips with some glue. A gentle finger tip squeeze on the ends of the ratline helps to secure them.

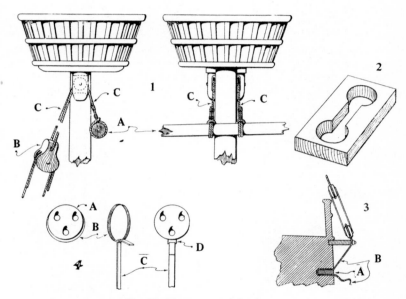

Fig. 33. Mast-tops and deadeyes

The orthodox method used in rattling down is to start opposite your left eye when looking inboard. In very large scales there is an eyesplice in the end of the ratline (at both ends in fact). Ratline is outside the rigging, and it is clove hitched on each shroud. If using a clove hitch on the ends (as is usually done in models) do not cut off too short but rub the end round the shroud with "tacky" fingers. Distance apart in modern ships (i.e., nineteenth and twentieth century windjammers) is, lower rigging, 14 in. ; topmast rigging, 15 in., and topgallant mast, 16 in., but 15 in. is safe for any period and position.

Sails, parts of a sail. Buntline cloths, tabling or hemming, middle-band. top pieces, reef-band, head, foot, leech, gore. Canvas is 22 in. wide. Seam 1 in, Sailcloths, therefore, are 21 in. centre to centre. Cloths are vertical in square sails. In the staysails and jibs, they are parallel to the foot and the leech respectively, meeting on a line which joins the clew to the centre of the luff.

Roping for a sail is on the after side of square sails and on the port side of fore-and-aft sails. The head of the sail has roping only half the diameter of that at the leech and foot. Push the needle *between* the top and two bottom strands to come out of the canvas about three-quarters of the diameter of the rope from the edge of the canvas. Now pull the "twine" back over the top of the canvas so that the twine lies naturally in the space or valley between the rope strands. Pull tight and repeat. The first few times you do it the rope will twist. Cut the twine and do it again *but allow for stretching the rope.* The good roping which results is well worth the trouble. Make your head and clew splices as late as possible, i.e., "rope" as much as you can before splicing. The wartime tin hat makes an excellent aid in giving a smooth belly to your "canvas." A very weak solution of gum or glue will "fix" your sails. The

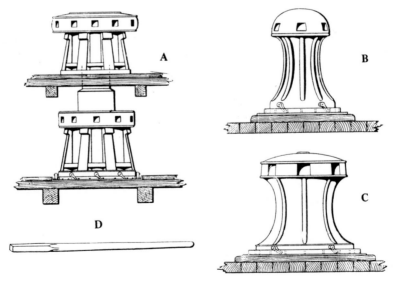

Fig. 34. Capstans

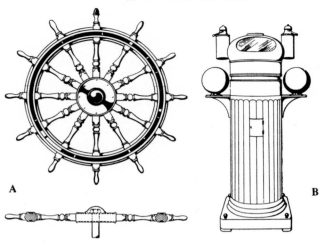

A   B

Fig. 35. Wheel and binnacle

modern windjammer master and even the packets and clippers knew the value of a flat sail. The " flowing curves " and the " billowy pyramids " are useless to the sailorman.

Changing the scale. Sometimes you have a set of plans but not to the scale you want. You want a model 18 in. long but the profile plan is $13\frac{1}{4}$ in. long. Here's how ! Referring to Fig. 37, draw a line parallel to the keel. Mark off (by perpendiculars) the length of the ship. From one end of the line draw a convenient line and divide into eighteen equal parts. This new line is a scale on which you can measure any part of your model. Transfer your drawing dimension to the upper line and read off your model size from the lower line. The lower line will be in parts equalling inches (eighteen of them). Divide one of the lower parts into fractions of an inch for your convenience.

SHROUDS, STAYS, BACKSTAYS, SPLICES, ETC.

Splicing. Thread each strand into a shortened darning needle. If the " ropes " are small just tuck the whole rope a couple of times and " finger " the " splice " with darkened beeswax or suitable glue.

Setting up shrouds. A good method to ensure that all deadeyes are taut, equally spaced between upper and lower deadeyes, and the shroud is bar-tight. Use a jig to hold the deadeyes. Reeve off the lanyard and make fast. Lay out the shrouds on paper, carefully measured, allowing for extra length for the after shrouds. Turn in the shrouds (i.e., cut them and seize them on to their upper deadeyes). Attach the " chains " to the lower deadeye. Now place

Fig. 36. A simple jig for making ladders

your shrouds over the mast head in proper order and plug the end of the chain into a hole below the channel. Cut off the superfluous plug. The plugging exerts that tightness which helps to " make " your model. Plug No. 1 Starboard, No. 1 Port, No. 2 Starboard, No. 2 Port.

Fig. 33/1 shows the method of hoisting the main yard in a ship of the fifteenth and sixteenth centuries. A is the yard ; B a ram headed block which may be two-fold or three-fold ; C is the tie, both ends being made fast to the yard. The ties run over the sheaves which are pivoted in cheeks on either side of the mast. Note the use of the seldom used cow hitch for securing the tie to the yard.

Tools. The dentist has many small chisels of various sizes and shapes. He discards them when past their prime for teeth, but modellers and carvers would be glad of them.

The dentist also has tiny drills and cutters of many shapes. In time they become second class for him, but first class (for many years) for modellers, especially if you have a flexible shaft drill. Of course, you can buy them new ! A good ship model society ought to have a dentist's drill.

Old files make excellent chisels, so do old and broken needles. Some modellers swear there is no better chisel than the broken hacksaw blade which has been sharpened. Run your eye over a manicure set of a good quality if you have any carving to do. There are excellent carving tools available. The dentist's drill is a wonderful affair, but you'll have to be *very* friendly with your dentist to gain access to his. There are dozens of different drills and, perhaps, if *you* supply the drills . . . . ?

A box of assorted entomological pins from Messrs. Watkins & Doncaster of Welling, Kent, would probably solve many difficulties of stanchions, flag poles, davits, etc. in some of the smaller scales. These are tough and very fine. Arterial forceps automatically grip and hold fast until released by a pressure of the fingers. There is also a smaller pair, the mosquito. They and other tools, are to be purchased from surgical Instrument Makers. Here's one firm, Messrs. Down Bros. & Mayer and Phelps Ltd., Church Path, Mitcham, Surrey. Square, London, W.1.

VENTILATORS AND COWLS

There are many ways of making ventilator cowls, but one man's meat is another man's poison. Here are some ideas which have proved successful.

Modellers should note that each of the shipbuilding localities had its own particular shape of cowl. Indeed, it was possible at a distance to say, " That's a Clyde-built ship," or, " She was built at Belfast," etc., etc. The sizes and shapes of ventilators have multiplied enormously since the beginning of the century. Although mechanical ventilation and air conditioning have made big strides, natural ventilation is still found on all kinds of ships. If in doubt about the exact appearance of your required ventilator, write to the owners or the builders. They usually have photographs or sketches.

In the following methods you must satisfy yourself as to the most suitable for work and for scale. Probably you'll work out a better method of your own.

First method : Cut off the conical protective cap usually supplied for covering the end of a pencil, obtainable at the cheap store stationery counters. Solder this to a piece of tubing of the right diameter. Then run a drill up inside the stem if required.

Second method : Using old briar pipes. Discard the mouthpiece. Scrape the bowl down with a penknife. Drill the stem to the required size. These are suitable for large scales only.

Third method : Use a lead former correctly shaped but very slightly under size. On this place a copper deposit (electrically) from a solution of copper sulphate (jam jar and torch battery). The lead former is melted out afterwards.

Fourth method : An iron or steel mould in two parts having a join vertically down the centre from the mouth of the cowl through to the back. Using soft copper wire pushed as far as it will go, there is ample soft copper to be beaten into the cowl shape. The mould may also include a rim for additional strength. These make surprisingly good ventilators. The snag is getting the mould made. This is a toolmaker's job. Good for scales up to $\frac{1}{8}$ in.

Fifth method : Lead beaten round a wooden former. I don't like this

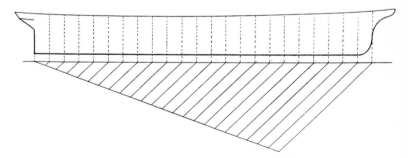

Fig. 37. Method of modifying the scale

method.   There has to be a seam somewhere to get the former out and *lead should never be used on a model.*

Sixth method. Plastic wood over wax. Some chaps like this method but I don't know why.

Seventh method : Turned in a lathe just like the making of a pipe. Suitable for big scales. Wood or metal.

Eighth method : Carving, just plain wood carving. The dentist's drill is a big help here.

Ninth method : Papier-mache (wet paper pulp and gum) in two formers, first the bowl, then dry ; add the stem stiffened by wire, then dry. Medium scales only.

Tenth method : Celluloid dissolved in amyl acetate painted over a waxed former in two pieces.

Club membership.

IN something like a dozen years I founded over a score of ship model societies in various parts of the world. My part of the work was really small, except in the case of the first few. I had much help from the Press, quite a lot of help from that bright little magazine, *Ships and Ship Models*, but the greatest help came from the prospective members themselves. *Every single modeller is a lone worker until he meets another lone modeller.* Then their troubles are halved and their progress is doubled. I have never met a modeller yet who has not found some simple device or trick in modelling which was new to a circle of a dozen modellers. Generally, one is good in woodwork, another in metals, another makes a good job of painting, and still another does miraculous work in rigging. It follows that if such men and women meet at regular intervals, bringing some samples of their craftsmanship *together with their troubles, failures, and obstacles*, the hours of a long evening will fly.

The foregoing is so obvious that I need not labour the matter here. THIS IS NOT SUFFICIENT. A meeting of three or four should formally form themselves into a ship model society, with a chairman, secretary and treasurer. Half-a-crown should be thrown into the kitty and a regular meeting night fixed either weekly or monthly. A few rules are necessary, but the fewer the better.

Certain rules are essential. They should be pledged to accuracy. They should endeavour to model a known or " named " ship and they should at least do some elementary research work sufficient to prevent anachronisms and to present a reasonably true picture of the ship-prototype.

Nor is this sufficient. A definite date should be fixed for the first annual exhibition of members' work. In the matter of this exhibition, it might be advantageous to join forces with a local model locomotive or aeroplane society. The large local store is always glad to allocate a corner of their store for a week. They may even throw in a prize or two, and your membership will increase thereby. For your second year you'll find liner companies will lend you a model or two and one or two local V.I.P.'s may be induced to come along.

There is added value, too, in the fact that a society will naturally get more attention than a few men following a kitchen table hobby. As time goes on it will be found that certain members specialise, all of which is to the general advantage of the society's prestige and standards. I found it a good practice when introducing a new member to the society to mention his special interest, period and type. It is still more important to introduce the members to the new entrant. At once he finds his opposite numbers and is " at home." Encourage the membership of artists. It is mutually advantageous. Invite the Press, especially on important nights. *Encourage the modelling of craft with a local interest.* This is common sense, for it breeds a helpful interest and valuable publicity. Contact other societies in adjacent parts. Visit the docks, or a famous ship, as an organised body and by arrangement with your hosts for the time being. Plan a trip to a shipping gallery or museum. I sometimes had four ship model societies together in Liverpool. Of course, the Mecca of all ship modellers is *The Model Engineer* Exhibition, in London.

A good society has a library. This is how it is done. No books are kept in a common library, but the librarian compiles a list of books owned by the members. Many of the books are, of course, commonplace and ordinary in the eyes of the experienced modeller, but there may be one or two outstanding or unusual books.

Already " librarians " of several ship model societies have contacted each other not only in the exchange of lists, but also to pass on tips as to where some of the rarer books are to be found. All beginners should keep away from the rarer books. They should be left for the " older hands " as much as possible, just because they are rare.

Well, we are near our landfall, and like the seamen in the windjammers, when they were taking a cast of the deep sea lead, we will yell out our warning from one to the other. We must not forget it, the cry of " Watch there, Watch," as the last flakes and coils leave our hands.

I've tried to guide you over 5,000 years and 5,000 ships, but all true seamen check their position when approaching the land, no matter how good their navigation may be. So watch there, watch ; be accurate, be definite, be gregarious. Yes, get into a herd for the sake of the improved standard of workmanship which is bound to result.

ACKNOWLEDGMENTS

It would be idle to pretend that this book is the work of one brain. It is not. In the preparation of the material now presented I have received the most generous help from a great many friends and authorities, far too many to be listed individually.

And so I ask their indulgence in the quandary in which I find myself, and simply record my very grateful thanks to all those who so kindly advised and assisted me in the compilation of this work.

Bibliography.

The following list of books and periodicals is suggested as a basis for your work in seeking information. It is reasonably exhaustive but obviously you will need only those titles which refer to the period in which you are interested. Do not accept the written word blindly. Check it, and check it carefully. The Society for Nautical Research, through its organ The Mariners' Mirror, keeps careful guard on all matters of the sea, ships, and sailors. There is your ultimate test if required, but be very sparing in your appeal there. It should be the supreme court, as it were. Much of what is sought by a novice can be cleared up at the average society meeting. A great deal more may be unearthed through your own local library. This list is for reference only.

Also, published during the last half century, on the subjects of house flags and funnels are four sheets, by the Journal of Commerce Liverpool, books by Brown, Son & Ferguson, Ltd., Glasgow, and Lloyd's House Flags and Funnels.

There are a considerable number of seamanship books and Admiralty Manuals of Seamanship which cover more than half-a-century of Merchant Navy and Royal Navy.

The following annuals, etc., must be mentioned: Lloyd's Calendar, Lloyd's Register Book, Jane's Fighting Ships, Transactions of the Royal Institution of Naval Architects. Publications of the Navy Records Society (published at intervals). Mariner's Mirror, the organ of the Society for Nautical Research, published quarterly. Museum handbooks, Illustrated Periodicals (back files). The National Reference Library is particularly useful to research workers. There is also a Records Office for Patents (18th and 19th century) under the control of the Librarians of our larger cities.

Finally, keep a cuttings record of pictures, photographs and clippings on your own chosen subject.

If you are a beginner don't spend money on books until you have chosen your particular subject. A talk with one of similar interests will be your best guide.

Abell, Sir Westcott The Shipwright's Trade 1948. *Shipbuilding Ancient and Modern.*

Albion, Prof. R.C. Naval & Maritime History, *A Bibliography 1963 4th Ed. 1972.*

Albion, Prof. R.C. Square-Riggers on Schedule: *The New York Sailing Packets to England, France and the Cotton Ports. 1938. R. 1965. Full tabular data on each vessel.*

Anderson R. & R.C. The Sailing Ship: *6,000 Years of History. 1926. R. 1963. The standard over-all work on sail.*

Anderson R. Rigging of Ships in the Days of the Spritsail Topmast. *1927. 17th and early 18th Century rigging.*

Archibald E.H.H. The Wooden Fighting Ship in the Royal Navy. *A.D. 897 – 1860. 1968.*

Aymar B A Pictorial Treasury of the Marine Museums of the World. *1967.*

Baker W.A. Colonial Vessels: *Some 17th Century Sailing Craft. 1962.*

Baker W.A. The New Mayflower: *Her Design and Construction by Her Designer. 1958.*

Biddlecombe Sir G. The Art of Rigging *1925.*

Bowen F.C. From Carrack to Clipper: *A Book of Sailing Ship Models. 1927.*

Bowen J.L. Waterline Ship Models. *1972.*

Bowling, Tom (P.Hodge). The Book of Knots. *1890. A Complete treatise on the art of cordage. R. 1969.*

Bowness E. The Four Masted Barque.

Bowness E. Modelling the Cutty Sark. *1959.*

Bonsor N.R.P. North Atlantic Seaway. *1955.*

Boyd Manual of Naval Construction. *1859. 19th Century Seamanship.*

Bugler A. H.M.S. Victory: *Building, Restoration and Repair. 1967.*

Bushnell A Complete Shipwright. *1669. Plans for a small ship.*

Carr F.G.G. Sailing Barges. *1931 R. 1951, 1971. The definitive history of these craft.*

Carr-Laughton Old Ships' Figureheads and Sterns. *1925.*

Chapelle H.I. The Baltimore Clipper *1930. R. 1969.*

Chapelle H.I. History of American Sailing Ships. *1935.*

Chapelle H.I. The National Watercraft Collection.*1960. Models in the Smithsonian Collection.*

Chapelle H.I. The Search for Speed Under Sail. *1700–1955. 1967.*

Chapman F.H. Architectura Navalis Mercatoria 1768. *R. 1820, 1935, 1957, 1967, 1971. Copious lines and draughts of 18th Century ships.*

Charnock J. A History of Marine Architecture. *3 vols. 1800–1802. A rambling miscellany.*

Chatterton E.K.	Ship Models. *1923*
Chatterton E.K.	Steamship Models. *1924*
Clowes, G.S. Laird	Sailing Ships, Their History and Development. *2 vols. 1930–1932. The collection of Ship Models in the Science Museum.*
Corbett J.	Papers relating to the Navy during the Spanish War, 1585–1587. *1898. Good material on Armada ships.*
D'Arcy Lever	The Young Sea Officer's Sheet Anchor, 1808, 1841. *R. 1937, 1968. Rigging and Seamanship.*
Davis C.G.	The Built-Up Ship Model. *1933. R. 1966.*
Deane, Sir A.	Doctrine of Naval Architecture 1670. *Body Plans & Rigging plans for 1st – 6th Rates.*
Dummer	Draughts of the Body of an English Man Of War. *1680.*
Encyclopaedia Britannica	11th Ed. 1911, 'Ships' and 'Shipbuilding'.
Falconer W.	A New and Universal Dictionary of the Marine. *1804. R. 1971.*
Falconer W.	The Old Wooden Walls. *An abridged edition of Falconer by C.S.Gill, 1930.*
Frere-Cook G.	The Decorative Arts of the Mariner. *1966*
Ffoulkes	Gunfounders of England. *1937.*
Fincham J.	Directions for Laying Off Ships on the Mould Loft Floor. *1822.*
Fincham J.	Treatise on Masting Ships and Mastmaking. *1829. 1851.*
Fincham J.	History of Marine Architecture. *1851.*
Fox Smith C.	Ship Models. *1951. R. 1972*
Hayward	Masts & Rigging. *1660. Sizes and lengths of rigging for all H.M. Ships and Frigates. Stuart Period.*
Hedderwick	Treatise on Marine Architecture. *1830*
Hobbs, E.H.	How to make Clipper Ship Models. *1927, and later editions.*
Holmes Sir G.	Ancient and Modern Ships. *Vol. I Sail, 1900. Vol. II Steam, 1906.*
Hutchinson Wm.	A Treatise on Naval Architecture. *1794. R. 1970. Not a 'how to do it' text, but a treatise on shipbuilding and seamanship.*
Isard Capt. A.R.	The Model Ship Builders Manual of Fittings and Guns. *1939.*
Isherwood J.H.	Steamers of the Past. *1966.*
Kipping R.	Sails and Sailmaking. *1857. Numerous editions to 1923. 71 Woodcuts.*
Kipping R.	Treatise on Masting, Mastmaking, and Rigging of Ships. *1851. Numerous editions to 1921. 135 woodcuts.*

Landstrom B. The Ship: *An Illustrated History. 1967. R. 1969*

Lindsay W.S. History of Merchant Shipping and Commerce, 1816–1874. *2 Vols. 70 illus. 1874.*

Longridge C.N. The Anatomy of Nelson's Ships. *1953.*

Longridge C.N. The Cutty Sark. *2 Vols. 1933. R. 1946.*

MacGregor D.R. The Hey-Day of Sail. *1815–1875. 1965.*

MacGregor D.R. The Tea Clippers. *1952. R. 1972.*

Mainwaring Sir H. The Seaman's Dictionary. *1644. R. Navy Records Society. 1922.*

March E.J. British Destroyers. *1893–1955. 1970.*

March E.J. Sailing Drifters. *1953. R. 1969.*

March E.J. Sailing Trawlers. *1953. R. 1969.*

March E.J. Spritsail Barges of Thames and Medway *1948. R. 1970.*

Masefield J. Sea Life in Nelson's Time. *1905. R. 1920, 1971. Useful chapters on ships' interiors, rigging and guns.*

Miller T. The Complete Modellist 1664. *Plates and tables on Rigging.*

Model Shipwright Quarterly Journal of Ships and Ship Models. *1st Vol. 1972.*

Moore Sir A The Last Days of Mast and Sail. *1925. R. 1970.*

Mountaine W. The Seaman's Vade Mecum. *1776. R. 1971. Gives proportions of rigging, masts, yards, cables, cordage of Navy Ships.*

Nares G.S. Seamanship. *1860. and subsequent editions.*

Needham J. Modelling Ships in Bottles. *1972.*

Norton P. The End of the Voyage. *1959.*

Paasch H. From Keel to Truck. *1885. Illustrating all parts of a ship. Captions in English, French, and German.*

Paasch H. Marine Encyclopaedia. *1890. Numerous plates.*

Paris, Vice Admiral Souvenirs de Marine. *1882. Accurate drawings of ships, ancient and modern.*

Parkes O. British Battleships. *1958. R. 1966, 1971.*

Pepys (Collection) Fragments of Ancient Shipwrightry. *Ca. 1586. Drawings of Elizabethan ships.*

Perrin W.G. British Flags. *1922. 13 cold plates.*

Petrejus E.W. Modelling the Brig-of-War 'Irene'. *A handbook for the building of historical ship models. 1970.*

Robertson F.L. Evolution of Naval Armament. *1921. R. 1968.*

Shetelig, Falk & Gordon Scandinavian Archaeology. *1937. Early boats of N.W. Europe.*

Steel D. Steel's Elements of Mastmaking, Sail-

	making and Rigging, (From the 1794 edition). *Arranged and with an introduction by C.S.Gill, 1958.*
Stewart C.L.	Flags, Funnels and Hull colours. *1953. R. 1963.*
Sutherland W.	Shipbuilders' Assistant. *1711.*
Talbot Booth E.C.	Merchant Ships. *Various editions since 1936.*
Talbot Booth E.C.	Waterline Ship Models. *1937.*
Todd & Whale	Practical Seamanship for use in the Mercantile Service. *1898.*
Underhill H.A.	Masting and Rigging the Clipper Ship and Ocean Carrier. *1947.*
Underhill H.A.	Deep Water Sail. *1952.*
Underhill H.A.	Plank on Frame Models. *2 Vols. 1958. R. 1971.*
Underhill H.A.	Sailing Ships and Rigging. *1956.*
United States Naval Academy Library	The Henry Huddleston Rogers Collection of Ship Models. *1954.*
Villiers A.	Last of the Windships. *1934. Photo illustrations of Windjammer sails, rigging and deck details.*
Warrington-Smith H.	Mast and Sail in Europe and Asia. *1906. R. 1971.*
Weyer's	Warships of the World. *1st English Ed. 1969.*

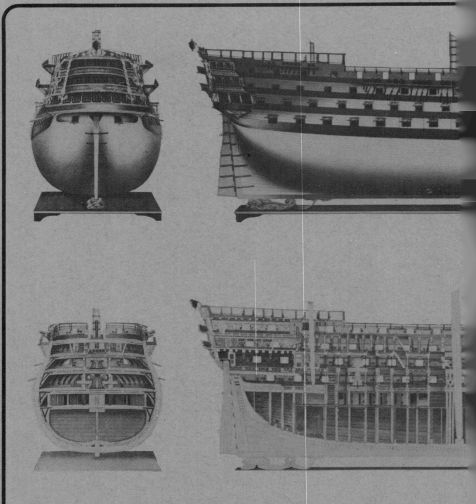

NELSON

Overall Length 244'0"
Breadth Extreme 53'8"
Length of the Keel 170'10"
Length on the Gun Deck 205'¾"
Burthen in tons 2617.4/94
Breadth Moulded 52'11"
Depth in Hold 24'0"

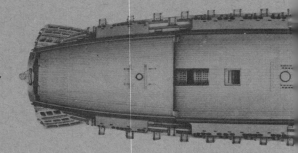